A STUDENT'S GUIDE TO
RELIGIOUS STUDIES

THE PRESTON A. WELLS JR.
GUIDES TO THE MAJOR DISCIPLINES

GENERAL EDITOR   EDITOR
JEFFREY O. NELSON   JEREMY BEER

PHILOSOPHY *Ralph M. McInerny*

LITERATURE *R. V. Young*

LIBERAL LEARNING *James V. Schall, S.J.*

THE STUDY OF HISTORY *John Lukacs*

THE CORE CURRICULUM *Mark C. Henrie*

U.S. HISTORY *Wilfred M. McClay*

ECONOMICS *Paul Heyne*

POLITICAL PHILOSOPHY *Harvey C. Mansfield*

PSYCHOLOGY *Daniel N. Robinson*

CLASSICS *Bruce S. Thornton*

AMERICAN POLITICAL THOUGHT *George W. Carey*

A Student's Guide to Religious Studies

D. G. HART

ISI BOOKS
WILMINGTON, DELAWARE

A Student's Guide to Religious Studies is made possible by grants from the Lee and Ramona Bass Foundation, the Lillian S. Wells Foundation, Barre Seid Foundation, and the Wilbur Foundation. The Intercollegiate Studies Institute gratefully acknowledges their support.

Library of Congress Cataloging-in-Publication Data:

Hart, D. G. (Darryl G.)

    A student's guide to religious studies / D. G. Hart — 1st ed. — Wilmington, Del. : ISI Books, c2005.

    p. ; cm.
    (ISI guides to the major disciplines)

    ISBN-13: 978-1-932236-58-3
    ISBN-10: 1-932236-58-9
    Includes bibliographical references.

    1. Religion—Study and teaching (Higher)—United States.
2. Education, Higher—Aims and objectives—United States.
3. Religious education—Philosophy. I. Title.

BL141 .H37 2005   2005921730
200/.7—dc22   0510

ISI Books
Intercollegiate Studies Institute
P.O. Box 4431
Wilmington, DE 19807-0431
www.isibooks.org

Design by Sam Torode

CONTENTS

For understanding is the recompense of faith. Therefore, seek not to understand so that you may believe, but believe that you may understand; for unless you believe, you will not understand.

— Saint Augustine, *Tractates on the Gospel of John*

INTRODUCTION

❧

"BELIEVE THAT YOU MAY UNDERSTAND." Over the centuries Saint Augustine's assertion about the relationship between religious belief and knowledge has inspired much reflection on faith's cognitive aspects. But his wisdom could prove frustrating to students hoping to understand religion better through the field of religious studies. As much as faith may benefit academic inquiry in many subjects, within the religion departments of most colleges and universities religious commitment is generally regarded as a barrier, rather than an asset, to understanding and wisdom. Believers are generally considered narrow- or close-minded and therefore incapable of investigating religious subjects in a neutral, objective, scientific manner.

Such prejudice against belief reflects not only the triumph of secularism in American higher education. Many factors have contributed directly to the suspicion with which personal faith is regarded in religious studies departments. Some of these factors will become apparent in the pages that follow. Certainly both the dominance and findings of the natural sciences during the last century have contributed to religion's decline in the university. Yet the rise of religious studies as an academic discipline also shaped the role that faith is usually allowed to play in the study of religion. Consequently, to understand the history and aims of the academic study of religion is important for students desiring to use such instruction and research for their own edification. Religious devotion is not likely to take one very far in most religion courses. At the same time, if students' expectations are appropriately modest in such classes, they may actually acquire tools that nurture both belief and understanding. After all, Saint Augustine's conviction about the priority of faith in knowledge does not exclude the necessity of acquiring wisdom through the kind of reading, critical thinking, and writing involved in the contemporary study of religion.

Of course, "faith seeking understanding" is not the only motivation for studying religion. Because Western civilization is unthinkable without the contributions of Judaism and Christianity, a desire for greater insight into the thinkers, artists, statesmen, and historical events shaping the West may also lead many students to take courses in religion departments. But disappointment may result even with this motivation, for the field of religious studies has generally followed the lead of other humanistic disciplines in adopting the view that Europeans—especially males—are responsible for the oppression of minorities, sexism, and an endless list of other cultural ills. In other words, the dominant perspective is that because Western civilization's most important religious texts and institutions were oblivious to contemporary notions of race, class, and gender, those texts and institutions should be approached with skepticism, if not outrage. Thus, if one enrolls in a religion course hoping to better understand and appreciate the religious ideals that fueled the West's artistic imagination, provided the basis for its philosophical insights, and informed its institutional and associational life, one should have realistic expectations about the probable prejudices of the professor.

Despite the disappointments that religious studies is sure to yield to the idealistic student, the academic discipline of religion nevertheless possesses resources that will truly benefit those hoping to acquire greater wisdom about the human condition or the contribution of faith to the West's development.

This guide is designed to help students navigate the study of religion in American higher education, to discover the best that our universities and colleges have to offer. First, we will explore the history of religion in American higher education, the rise of religious studies as an academic discipline, and several characteristic features resulting from this complicated history. Then we will recommend the best ways to approach the West's greatest religious thinkers and most significant texts. If students approach the academic study of religion understanding this background and with realistic goals, religious studies may prove a hospitable environment for faith and understanding not only to coexist, but to flourish.

I. THE UNIVERSITY'S RELIGIOUS ROOTS

THE MYTH OF CHRISTIAN
HIGHER EDUCATION IN AMERICA

America's most prestigious universities have their origins in the colonial era (roughly 1600 to 1775), a time when religion held a prominent place in the nation's public and intellectual life. Harvard and Yale, for instance, were founded under the auspices of New England's Puritans, while Princeton started chiefly with the support of mid-Atlantic Presbyterians. Thus, the best universities in America emerged for explicitly religious reasons, with the training of clergy a primary rationale for undergraduate education. Even after the American Revolution and ecclesiastical disestablishment, the needs and beliefs of religious bodies continued to shape higher education in the United States. As the new nation spread across the continent, denominational colleges sprang up everywhere Americans sought higher learning. These colleges featured a liberal education with a decidedly Christian ethos. The church's influence was felt, for example, in the standard senior-year capstone course in moral philosophy. The college president—invariably a minister—would integrate the entire undergraduate curriculum while also vindicating Christianity's truth and the necessity of religion for the good society.

If American undergraduate education was intentionally Christian during the colonial and antebellum (1800 to 1860) eras, it appeared to diverge considerably from its historic character with the advent of the research university, a development that significantly altered American learning during the post–Civil War decades. This "revolution" in higher education severed America's colleges from their Christian roots and established as the goal of learning training in the methods and specialized research of the natural and social sciences.

Big business—as opposed to the churches—was responsible for the founding of most of the new research universities. Cornell (1865), Johns Hopkins (1876), Stanford (1885), and the University of Chicago (1890) were made possible only by drawing on the fortunes of leading industrialists. At the same time, older institutions started to abandon the religious rules that governed their procedures for hiring and recruiting in order to attract the funding that the new learning required. Higher education became more expensive in part because of the new subjects it incorporated; to keep pace colleges needed to add courses and faculty in the natural and social sciences. Additionally, the specialization of academic disciplines created the need for even more courses and faculty; the course in moral philosophy, for instance, had covered ground that would later require courses in philosophy, sociology, history, anthropology, and ethics—at least. Suitable faculty became harder to find because of the increased demand for specialists in concentrated areas of study.

Indeed, one of the most significant changes wrought by the rise of the research university was the professionalization of knowledge. Unlike the previous era, when the learned gentleman (most often a minister) could teach a variety of subjects in the undergraduate curriculum, in the research university (and in the colleges that sought to emulate them) scholars specialized in narrow fields of study as experts. What the colonial and denominational colleges may have lacked in cutting-edge scholarship they made up for in their attempt to integrate a whole range of knowledge from a religiously informed perspective. Thus, curricular integration was now sacrificed for the sake of intellectual expertise.

These changes in American higher education have fueled the plausible notion that colleges and universities began to secularize after 1870. To be sure, the place of religion at the new research universities (and at those liberal arts colleges that tried to keep up with them by following the path of academic specialization) was noticeably different. Chapel usually became voluntary, religious tests for faculty hiring generally faded away, and the sense that the churches were the rightful proprietors of higher learning gradually evaporated thanks both to the new ideals to which administrators and faculty adhered and to new sources of funding. What is less credible in this generally accurate portrait of late-nineteenth-century American higher education is the notion that the denominational colleges undermined by the research universities had been bastions of Christian higher education in the first place. As friendly as the colonial and denominational colleges were to faith—and it should be remembered that since the churches were their patrons the colleges did not really have a choice—the explicitly religious content of their undergraduate curricula was minimal. Those who maintain that our colleges and universities need to return to an older pattern in which religion was central to higher learning need to revise their arguments. Formal religious study has always been more or less marginal to American higher education. To look, then, to religious studies as a means of recovering an older Christian-centered vision of higher education is both to misunderstand the achievements of the past and to constrain the possibilities of the future.

THE ERA OF THE CHRISTIAN COLLEGE

Many of the difficulties faced today by those who study religion in American higher education stem from the English and Protestant precedents that the British colonists in North America followed when establishing colleges in the New World. For the British Protestants who founded colleges in Massachusetts (e.g., Harvard) and Virginia (e.g., William and Mary), formal instruction in the Christian religion—that is, the study of Scripture and theology—was almost exclusively reserved for those training for the Christian ministry. Such theological education was not part of British university instruction even for those who would become clergy. (Not until the nineteenth century did British colleges and universities establish faculty posts in explicitly religious subjects.) Prospective ministers needed to have university training, but their education was a primarily literary one that provided a familiarity with ancient languages, texts, and authors. For theological instruction, students would supplement their university education with apprenticeships completed under the supervision of settled ministers. Here is where future pastors would become better acquainted with church teaching, biblical interpretation, and ecclesiastical polity, and where they would gain firsthand experience of parish life. This same pattern prevailed in the New World, where the colonial colleges included religious training sufficient to maintain a godly society but insufficient to prepare students for the ministry. For the formal theological education necessary for ordination, prospective ministers typically needed training beyond college.

The lack of formal theological instruction in undergraduate education helps to explain why prior to the nineteenth century leading theological scholars were more often pastors than professors. Take Jonathan Edwards, considered by many to be the greatest American theologian. Edwards's training and ecclesiastical appointments were fairly typical of the time, even if his scholarly output was remarkable. He was a graduate of Yale College and apprenticed with his grandfather in Northampton, Massachussetts, before being ordained and succeeding his grandfather as pastor of that congregation. As a defender of the First Great Awakening, Edwards established a reputation as both a devout pastor and a learned theologian who was able to use philosophy to justify religious revivals. Still, all of Edwards's literary output took place on the frontier of colonial society—a small town in western Massachusetts, not in a faculty office at Harvard or Yale. In fact, some of Edwards's most important theological works were produced after a conflict with his Northampton congregation forced him to accept a call to mission work among nearby Native Americans. Because of Edwards's reputation as a pastor and scholar, a network of congregations and pastors developed along the Connecticut River Valley that became known as the New Divinity. This informal association depended on the apprenticeship model of theological training. Most of the New Divinity network's members had at one time studied with Edwards and served as an intern in his congregation; in turn, these Edwards students took on apprentices who would also become part of the New Divinity theological tradition.

Edwards's own literary output, as well as his establishment of an informal school (or tradition) of theology, underscores the place of formal religious instruction during the colonial era. As difficult as his own personal circumstances may have been, Edwards's distance from an academic institution was not unusual, because the best formal American scholarship in theology and the Bible was produced by pastors like him. At the same time, the cultivation and preservation of a particular pattern of religious training flourished best outside the colonial colleges. The formal study of religion was chiefly an activity for the churches, which not only provided the training future ministers needed before ordination, but also resolved the various disputes arising within religious communions. The study of religion was a fairly technical field of inquiry not regulated directly by the institutions of American higher education. Of course, it clearly was important to colonial society. But even so, formal religious study was not part of a classical education and so had no home in the colleges and universities.

A similar pattern would prevail in the denominational liberal arts colleges founded by churches in the nineteenth century. These institutions were clearly Christian in character, but the curriculum continued to be dominated by Greek and Latin, and knowledge of the ancient world was supposed to provide the basis for understanding, wisdom, and virtue. Aside from the senior-year course in moral philosophy, which acquainted students with the demands of Christian conduct and evidences for the truth of Christianity, the denominational college's curriculum made little room for the formal study of the sacred scriptures and theology.

Religion's academic fortunes began to change in the nineteenth century with the advent of the theological seminary. Congregationalists in New England started Andover

Theological Seminary in 1808 and Presbyterians followed suit in 1812 with Princeton Theological Seminary, thus signaling the decline of the older apprentice model of ministerial training. Seminaries provided a more efficient way to train ministers for the rapidly expanding nation. In turn, the faculty at these institutions, all ministers themselves, eventually acquired the status of theological experts whose full-time job was religious study and inquiry; unlike Edwards and his like, they were not required to combine their scholarship with pastoral responsibilities. During the nineteenth century almost every church founded its own seminary or added a divinity school to an existing college, as was the case with Harvard and Yale. In the late nineteenth century, when the research university was rising to prominence, the divinity-school model became increasingly common. The University of Chicago, Emory, Vanderbilt, and Duke all added their divinity schools during these years.

But as much as the creation of seminaries and divinity schools may have helped to improve the academic credentials of religious studies, formal instruction in the Bible and theology continued to be a sphere of inquiry set apart from the arts and sciences. Theological education, even in its more professional setting, was still reserved for ministerial preparation. It was not regarded to have special relevance for, or applicability to, the humanities or sciences. The marginal standing of theological education within American learning was a source of great consternation to seminary and divinity school faculty. Thus, during the late nineteenth and early twentieth centuries various plans were put forth to overhaul theological education. Such undertakings usually sought to bring theological study into the mainstream of American higher education and to train ministers who would be better equipped to address the concerns of America's rapidly industrializing and urbanizing society. Ironically, this attempt to improve the standing of theological education actually reinforced the perception that formal instruction in the Bible and theology were subjects far removed from the *regular* arts and sciences, from the *real* world.

Theological educators, in fact, did not propose to reform ministerial training by demonstrating the importance of biblical exegesis or systematic theology to the pursuit of knowledge and wisdom. Instead, it was a prominent notion in the seminaries and divinity schools of the late nineteenth and early twentieth centuries that religion, given the chance, could, like other fields of learning, contribute to society's improvement. This was the era of the Social Gospel, when the mainline Protestant churches sought to demonstrate faith's relevance to everyday life by lending support to numerous social reforms designed to offset the lamentable side-effects of large-scale industrialization and urbanization. Church leaders also professed to discern in social and cultural developments signs of the kingdom of God. The net effect for the study of religion was to shift ministerial training away from theology and the Bible to include more instruction in the natural and social sciences. The natural sciences, it was thought, would help ministers answer objections from skeptics who doubted divine control of the evolutionary process. The social sciences would prepare future clergy to channel religious vitality into those various reforms which sought to preserve Christian influence in America's fast-changing cities.

Some university presidents welcomed these changes in theological education, believing that they heralded a new and better day for the churches. In fact, it was during this era (1880–1930) that religious studies arguably reached its nadir as an academic discipline. The creation of seminaries and divinity schools had provided theological education with an institutional foothold in the academic world, but these theological schools could not withstand the challenge presented by the new learning of the research university. Consequently, in trying to show the relevance of religion to other fields of study, theological educators, paradoxically, accomplished precisely the opposite: they brought the new knowledge of the research university to bear on religion. Instead of specializing in their own fields of inquiry (i.e., the subdisciplines of theology, scriptural exegesis, etc.), theological educators dabbled as generalists in fields for which they were ill equipped. On the eve of the twentieth century, the prospects for religious studies in American higher education looked bleak, not simply because of the threat posed by secularization, but also, and perhaps more decisively, because of religion's historically marginal status in the nation's colleges and universities.

THE UNIVERSITY GETS RELIGION

The study of religion in American higher education today may not be central to the missions of the leading colleges and universities. But religious studies is no longer merely the preoccupation of prospective ministers and theological educators. In fact, the study of religion is one of the largest enterprises in American learning. The American Academy of Religion—the professional academic organization responsible for setting standards in the field of religious studies—counts over 8,000 members who teach at more than 1,500 colleges and universities. At first, this seems a surprising turn of events. Religious studies' popularity is less startling, however, once the circumstances under which it achieved academic respectability are understood better. The study of religion had to meet specific conditions to gain legitimacy in the mainstream of American learning.

Protestants of English descent took the lead in positioning religion as an academic subject within American higher education. Of course, ethnic Protestants, Roman Catholics, and Jews were all interested in the study of their faiths. But for religious studies to prevail as a respectable partner in the American intellectual endeavor it would need a plausible rationale to those both outside and within the household of faith. Mainline Protestants, because of their own privileged status as part of America's unofficial religious establishment, were best equipped to devise such an argument. Furthermore, mainstream Protestants' commitment to the project of preserving Christian civilization required them to try, no matter how clumsily, to combine the private demands of faith with the public requirements of civil society—or, in this case, the public requirements of free and open inquiry in the classroom and at the study carrel.

The Protestant strategy for gaining a foothold for religious studies in American higher education drew first upon the churches' ministerial, as opposed to intellectual, resources. Many Protestant church leaders in the early twentieth century worried about the secular drift in American higher education, particularly at state universities. They responded by establishing a variety of extracurricular organizations designed to foster students' piety. The precedent for such a strategy had been set in the last decades of the nineteenth century, when the Young Men's Christian Association, the Young Women's Christian Association, and the Student Volunteer Movement became prominent features of campus life. By conducting Bible studies, sponsoring public lectures on religious subjects, and providing wholesome forms of sociability, these interdenominational Protestant associations were principle sources for the religious inspiration of college students. Another important component of religious instruction was chapel. Though major universities like Harvard, Cornell, and Johns Hopkins made attendance at daily worship services voluntary, most institutions—from state universities to denominational colleges—continued to require chapel attendance for their undergraduates.

In the first two decades of the twentieth century the inadequacy of these extracurricular organizations had become clear. Therefore, Protestants embarked upon a program of founding university pastorates and Bible chairs at large state and private universities. The ministers who staffed these offices had the task of ensuring the religious well-being of students from their own denominations. Presbyterians, Congregationalists, Baptists, Methodists, Lutherans, Episcopalians, and Disciples of Christ all followed this model. University pastors not only conducted Sunday services and Bible studies but also were expected to participate in the life of the university and to encourage students to consider careers in the ministry. They also offered Bible instruction and denominational teaching either at churches or at denominational centers adjacent to campus. Although these courses were not part of the college or university curriculum, church leaders worked with university administrators so that students could receive official credit for this sort of training. Eventually, Roman Catholics and Jews adopted this model as well, especially at state universities, and teaching courses in religion became a regular part of a university pastor's responsibilities.

As successful as these extracurricular efforts may have been in providing a religious presence on campus (or at least nearby), until the 1940s religion as an academic subject remained on the periphery of American learning. Part of the trouble was the older association of theology and biblical study with professional education for the ministry, at best, or with the catechetical training (or "indoctrination") of church members, at worst. Furthermore, there did not seem to be a natural affinity between religion and the other disciplines in the arts and sciences. This was especially the case in the 1920s, when the distinct identities of the social sciences and humanities were so pronounced that a hostile rivalry developed. When the American Council of Learned Societies Dedicated to Humanistic Studies (later simply the ACLS) was founded in 1919, its goal was to encourage "the philological, archaeological, historical, moral, political and social sciences" in much the same fashion that the National Research Council was already doing for the natural sciences. But instead of fostering intellectual collaboration, the ACLS actually drove the humanities and the social sciences apart by revealing their fundamental differences. By 1923, leaders in the social sciences had formed a separate organization, the Social Science Research Council. The chief impetus for the division was the widespread belief that the scientific method, employed best by natural scientists, was the only legitimate way for social scientists to provide credibility to their own study of human relations. The result was that the humanities gained a reputation for being "soft"; they dealt with spiritual or abstract matters that could not be measured and so were not genuinely scientific.

In Search of an Academic Niche

For church officials and university pastors hoping to secure a place for religion in the college curriculum, the rivalry between the social sciences and humanities might have yielded a clear path. The division between spiritual or idealistic matters and the world of facts and data may have meant that religion had no opportunity to be a science, but it could at least join the enterprise of advanced learning as a humanistic field of study. The problem was that most academics thought religion was more naturally an ally of the social sciences. Because the perception—largely facilitated by Protestants—was that a primary role of religion involved promoting harmonious social relations, academics naturally perceived religious studies as having a greater affinity with the social sciences than with the humanities.

Not until the 1940s did religious studies' natural ties to the humanities become widely perceived. Professors of religion had begun during the 1930s to argue for their subject's importance on the grounds that it was a precious part of the West's cultural heritage. But, more importantly, during World War II many American educators came belatedly to recognize that science and secularism could not sustain the culture and values of liberal democracy. Beginning around 1940, a spate of books appeared that regarded the health of the "humanities" as an especially urgent question. The humanities were extolled because of their capacity to elevate, humanize, and instill ethical principles. Consequently, the prestige of the humanities grew among administrators and faculty, who began to implement curricular reforms that would give students a greater familiarity with the basis of the humane values of Western Europe and North America.

This pronounced concern for humanistic studies coincided with the increased attention being given to the need for more generalized studies. Harvard University's report,

General Education in a Free Society (1945), and the President's Commission on Higher Education's *Higher Education for American Democracy* (1948) exemplified the new effort to employ the humanities in the United States' battle with totalitarianism. Each of these influential proposals conflated older conceptions of the humanities and liberal education with the idea of "general education." Each also criticized the emphasis on specialized research that had dominated American higher education since the late nineteenth century as a significant factor in the fragmentation of college education, which in turn was responsible for pervasive indifference to the ideals of liberty and democracy in the West. Consequently, these reports' authors argued for a general education curriculum that would acquaint students with the religion and culture of Western civilization. In the words of the President's Commission, general education should enable the student "to identify, interpret, select, and build into his own life those components of his cultural heritage that contribute richly to understanding and appreciation of the world in which he lives." Likewise, the Harvard report placed the cultural heritage of the West at the center of the curriculum so that students would be confronted with "a received idea of the good." For those advocating reform of American higher education, the humanities suddenly became indispensable, while the rhetoric of general education linked the humanities to those subjects which promoted humane, moral, spiritual, and liberal ideals.

Calls for curricular reform and coherence provided the advocates of religious studies with an opening for making religion a standard area of study for undergraduates. Religion was now a natural ally of the humanistic project to study spiritual, moral, and humane values. And the Christian religion in particular was now acknowledged to lie at the heart of the West's cultural development. Consequently, a number of Protestant leaders stepped forward to address the crisis of liberal democracy generated by World War II and the Cold War, the need for American higher education to respond to this crisis, and the capacity of religious studies to supply the spiritual dimension that American learning had been missing thanks to its infatuation with science and specialized research.

One of the first to argue for the academic study of religion during this period was William Adams Brown, professor of theology at the prestigious Union Theological Seminary. His book, *The Case for Theology in the Univer-*

sity (1938), was written as a response to a highly influential book by University of Chicago president Robert Maynard Hutchins titled *The Higher Learning in America* (1936). In his book, Brown unraveled an argument that attempted to show the superiority of theology to philosophy and implicitly positioned religion as one of the most important humanistic disciplines. He agreed with Hutchins that American higher education lacked intellectual coherence, but unlike Hutchins he believed religion offered the proper remedy for this problem.

Brown blamed the impoverished state of American higher education on two primary factors. The first was the churches' abandonment of the university by establishing seminaries and divinity schools wherein the study of religion was separated from the other branches of human investigation and learning. The second factor contributing to the university's intellectual incoherence was the educational reforms of the late nineteenth century that emphasized and rewarded academic specialization. As a consequence, academics in different disciplines had gone their own ways, with little concern for synthesis and the significance of their learning for the whole of human understanding.

The remedy for this fragmentation, from Brown's perspective, was not philosophy, as Hutchins had proposed, but theology. Philosophy failed because it could not generate "faith in a meaningful world." Theology, on the other hand, could restore intellectual unity because it accounted for a creator who imparted moral and spiritual order to the universe and, thus, provided a basis for individual virtue and common social purpose. Brown admitted that several of the world's faiths could supply such a coherent theological vision, but in the West generally, and in the United States specifically, Christianity suited this purpose uniquely well because it lay "at the heart of our Western culture."

The sort of Christianity that Brown had in mind, however, was rather timid. In its tenets it could not appeal to external authority or divine revelation, the cardinal mistakes of Roman Catholics and Protestant fundamentalists. Instead, it needed to be scientific in its approach. Historical investigation, for instance, could show that Christianity was crucial to the development of the West and particularly to liberal democracy. Theology could also show that God was "the basic reality in the universe and hence the key to the understanding of nature and of man." In effect, Brown's conception of religion was as a propaedeutic to knowledge. In other words, if the human mind's composition and the universe's knowability depended on a creator who had so ordered man's reason and the cosmos, theology could supply the intellectual integration that American colleges and universities desperately needed.

Brown's colleague at Union, Henry P. Van Dusen, offered a similar argument in his 1951 book *God in Education*. But World War II and the initial stages of the Cold War imparted a greater sense of urgency to Van Dusen's argument. He believed that conducting science and education apart from religious considerations had been in some measure responsible for the destruction and hostilities in which the United States had been, and continued to be, engaged. For Van Dusen, Western civilization was moribund, and its only hope for recovery lay in moral and theological renewal.

According to Van Dusen, American universities were emblematic of the West's demise. Because higher learning had relied so heavily on empirical methods, the professoriate had excluded religious and moral considerations from scholarship. The introduction of religion as an academic subject, therefore, would serve to check the West's downward spiral. Van Dusen wrote that the "major purpose" of the emerging field of religious studies was "to introduce larger unity, coherence and therefore meaning, into the undergraduate's course of study." But merely adding religion courses was not enough. What the university needed was "a fundamental reorientation of *every* subject in the curriculum and its presentation in every course." "If there be a God at all," Van Dusen advised, "He must be the ultimate and controlling Reality through which all else derives its being; and the truth concerning Him, as man can best apprehend it, must be the keystone of the ever-incomplete arch of human knowledge." Van Dusen acknowledged that his proposal might appear to be at odds with the separation of church and state. But if public schools included prayer and Bible reading in their daily exercises, so also could the public space of American higher education make room for religious studies.

THE PROFESSIONALIZATION OF RELIGIOUS STUDIES
The pervasiveness of sentiments like those articulated by Brown and Van Dusen was widespread, and nearly everyone who wrote in such a vein proposed that religion be admitted to the university as an academic discipline. That wish was granted. During the two decades after World War

II the number of undergraduate programs in religion increased almost 100 percent, rising from twenty to thirty-eight. In addition, enrollment figures show that courses in religion attracted more students during the postwar years than did courses in any other area of study. Undergraduate enrollment in religion expanded most rapidly at private nonsectarian institutions. The number of students entering graduate programs of religion also increased dramatically. Between 1945 and 1960, sixteen North American institutions established programs leading to a doctorate in religious studies, an increase of approximately 60 percent. Meanwhile, the number of doctorates awarded during the 1950s more than tripled the number granted during the 1940s.

Another indication of religion's emerging prestige was given by the survey of humanistic scholarship commissioned by Princeton University's Council of the Humanities in the 1960s. Of the thirteen volumes covering disciplines as diverse as Chinese painting and philosophy, academic religion accounted for two of the entries, Clyde Holbrook's *Religion: A Humanistic Field* (1963), and *Religion* (1965), a collection of essays on the different fields in religion. Although religious scholarship had yet to be recognized by America's learned societies, the decision to devote two volumes of the Princeton Council's series to religion was the culmination of mid-twentieth-century academic interest in restoring meaning and purpose to higher education. The Princeton studies also revealed the links between the Protestant curriculum of most religious studies programs and the humanistic rationale for including religion in American higher education. *Religion,* edited by Princeton ethicist Paul Ramsey, consisted of chapters corresponding roughly to the prevailing Protestant seminary curriculum. The chapter on the history of religions, a relatively recent addition to theological education, was the only mention of non-Western systems of belief. Meanwhile, Holbrook, who taught religion at Oberlin College, used his monograph to summarize three decades of American Protestant thought about religion and higher education. The crucial issue was whether religious scholarship was a "liberalizing and humanizing area of instruction and scholarship." Obviously a complex question, Holbrook believed that religious studies was most fruitfully conducted in a humanistic context, because the study of religion made "available to the present the worthy embodiments of man's creativity."

These efforts to rescue American higher education from the dangers of specialization and secularization through the study of religion resulted in a curriculum well suited to Protestant interests. In fact, on most campuses the course of study closely resembled that found in Protestant seminaries and divinity schools. In part, this was the natural consequence of the fact that religion faculty had invariably studied at seminary or divinity schools, the only institutions heretofore granting doctorates in religion. But it also reflected the background of religious studies' greatest advocates, namely, the leaders of the mainline Protestant churches. Except for Roman Catholic and Jewish institutions, at most colleges and universities—whether public, private, or church-related—courses in the Old and New Testaments became the focal point of instruction in religion, while church history, theology, and ethics filled out the program. Faculty did often offer courses in comparative religion, but non-Christian religions were usually studied as partial expressions of the fuller truth revealed in Christianity. Few educators questioned the Protestant orientation of the curriculum because these courses seemed to provide an understanding of important aspects of Western civilization and American culture. Advocates for religious studies moved back and forth freely between "intellectual coherence" arguments (courses in religion provided needed integration to schools' badly fragmented curricula) and humanistic appeals (religion was fundamental to the West's cultural heritage).

As long as Protestant hegemony in the United States was maintained without serious controversy, this configuration of religious studies worked well. But this period was short-lived, ending with the various protest movements unleashed during the 1960s. Brown and Van Dusen had both been aware of the awkwardness of teaching Protestant Christianity in a religiously mixed and public forum. Religion's oddness became even more pronounced once important institutions in the United States took steps to deny the privileges previously granted to Protestantism. The most formal challenge to the study of religion came from the Supreme Court rulings in 1962 and 1963 that judged prayer and Bible reading in public schools to be unconstitutional. Although the justices distinguished devotional activity from the study of religion, the Court's decisions still signaled that Protestant dominance in American public life was coming to an end. No longer would it be possible to identify the "American way" with the faith of

America's oldest Protestant denominations, nor would Protestantism be synonymous with religion. Within just two decades after its most vigorous growth, religious studies would need to find another justification for participating in American higher education.

The most likely alternative for the academic study of religion in a post-Protestant America was to move away from the seemingly parochial orientation of religious (that is, Protestant) studies and strive for more inclusive configurations. This is exactly what happened. First, a professional scholarly society for religion faculty was organized, one comparable, for instance, to the Modern Language Association or the American Political Science Association. The leaders of religious studies created the American Academy of Religion (AAR) in 1964 to promote and informally regulate the academic discipline of religion. This was not a new organization. Rather, its 1964 incarnation represented a change of name for an older association, the National Association of Biblical Instructors, which was formed in 1909 as the professional society for Protestant campus ministers and teachers of religion in prep schools. This organization's moniker was obviously inadequate for serious academic inquiry into religion. The new name, on the other hand, indicated that the study of religion would no longer be preoccupied with religious questions within the United States ("American" instead of "National"), that it would be professionally rigorous ("Academy" instead of "Instructors"), and that it would include faiths other than Christianity ("Religion" instead of "Biblical"). The emergence of the AAR meant that religion professors would no longer be in the business of *promoting* religion (for either personal or civic purposes) but would rather be allowed to engage it *adversarially*, especially those faiths (such as Protestantism) that had been privileged in the curriculum and in Western society.

The other indication from this period that religious studies was acquiring a more scholarly and less religious character came from a report titled *Graduate Education in Religion: A Critical Appraisal* (1971). Written by Claude Welch, then a professor at the University of Pennsylvania, and cosponsored by the AAR and the American Council of Learned Societies, this study argued that the future for religious studies lay not in its ministerial aspirations but in its ability to produce specialized research. Implicit in this new emphasis on scholarship was a renewed interest in religion as a social science. The report surveyed the study of religion in North American colleges, universities, and seminaries and made recommendations for religious studies to achieve the academic stature necessary for the AAR to qualify for institutional membership in the ACLS. Welch argued that religious studies needed to move away from the dominance of "scriptural texts" and "*normative ideas*"(his emphasis). The field needed instead anthropological, sociological, and phenomenological studies that dealt "with the actual ways in which people act and believe." Welch also urged that more attention should be given to religious traditions other than Judaism and Christianity. "The time has come," he wrote, "when the parochialism of restricting religious studies to a single tradition can no longer be afforded." Finally, the report blamed the inferior state of religious studies on the dominance of Protestant seminaries and divinity schools in the training of PhDs. Welch advised creating new graduate programs at state and nonreligious private universities, where more scientific techniques for studying religion could be implemented.

In 1979 the ACLS admitted the AAR into its institutional membership. In doing so the academic study of religion became a recognized partner in American learning.

But such scholarly recognition came with a hefty cost. The academic certification of religious studies obscured the field's history and so prevented its practitioners from coming to terms with the field's Protestant, humanistic, and Cold War origins. Instead, with little historical reflection, religious studies assumed a new identity in the last decades of the twentieth century, one that seemingly yielded a blank slate upon which to create religion classes for undergraduates and advanced programs of study for future religion faculty. The new, scientific study of religion—complete with its own PhD—may have persuaded other scholars that religious studies was simply another of the university's many fields of advanced inquiry. But the history of the academic discipline of religious studies, from its ministerial origins and alliance with the humanities to its mid-twentieth-century role in buttressing the West, raised a series of important intellectual problems—problems that appeals to scientific standards could not settle. To those difficulties we now turn.

II. THE ACADEMIC PROBLEM
WITH RELIGION

❧

WHY STUDY RELIGION?

To understand the history of religion's emergence as an academic discipline in the United States is crucial for recognizing the likely strengths and weaknesses of religion courses in the contemporary university. Religion faculty, even the most devout, are bound by a constellation of professional expectations that prevent instruction in religious material from providing the sort of edification or inspiration that some students desire. At the same time, students approaching religion classes hoping to learn more about the role of faith in shaping the West need to be aware that religious studies once tried to fulfill that task in a triumphalist way. Partly as a reaction to that sort of narrow reading, today's religion courses tend to be critical of both faith and the West. Students have much to learn even from these critical approaches to religion, but it is better to be forewarned.

During the last decade or so religion has reemerged as a controversial subject in discussions about the state of American higher education. Several well-known scholars published books arguing that colleges and universities in the United States were unfairly predisposed to discount if not belittle religion.[1] In part, this is because universities discriminate against religious believers in their hiring practices. But the prejudice against religion goes even further, according to this line of criticism. Even if believing academics manage to be appointed, rules (usually unstated) restrict these professors from expressing their religious convictions in the classroom, office, committee, or department meeting. Yet, at the same time, virtually any nonreligious idea or opinion, no matter how bizarre or tasteless, is tolerated on today's campuses. Furthermore, if women, minorities, and homosexuals are welcomed to discuss essential aspects of their identities as such in the classroom, why should those academics for whom faith is at the heart of their self-understanding and calling have to censor themselves? In other words, this criticism of the bias against religion in American higher education appeals not only to widely accepted notions of cultural diversity but also to the ideal of academic freedom—the First Amendment, as it were, of the modern university.

Another complaint lodged by religionists against the contemporary academy is that the exclusion of religion decreases the quality of the education students receive. This argument focuses on religion's neglect in the curriculum. Those who take this line of criticism provide evidence, for instance, that survey courses in the history of the United States fail to account for religion's prominence not simply in colonial America but also at such watershed moments in national history as the abolitionist and Civil Rights movements. There is sometimes an element of religious boosterism in this approach, but it is made plausible by the many undeniably one-sided treatments of religion that treat faith only as an incubator of intolerance, bigotry, and cruelty. Whatever the merits of religion in the history of civilization, the bottom line is that a full and well-rounded education would not exclude one of the most basic components of human experience.

Finally, some thinkers pursue a religious version of the postmodern critique of the Enlightenment's biased and selective understanding of scientific objectivity. This argument proceeds as follows: One of the more important consequences of opening the academy to minority groups previously denied access was a recognition that the universal truths and methods studied and taught in the university were, in fact, the truths and methods of a particular, even parochial, subset of persons, namely, white men of European descent. As much as this recognition has been responsible for the abandonment of academic standards, it has also registered an important point. The Enlightenment's quest for truth was essentially an abstraction that failed to acknowledge the importance of the knower's situatedness as a member of a particular family, religion, and era, to name just a few of the circumstances that color all knowledge. Despite the temptation to relativize all claims to truth, this critique of Enlightenment rationality and individualism has led to a greater awareness that the notion of the autonomous individual, free from the prejudices of blood, land, and creed, is itself a form of prejudice rooted in particular social and cultural locations. In other words, as much as the Enlightenment framework for knowledge tried to escape the dogmatism that had governed learning prior to the era of modern science, it could not free itself from its own form of dogma, one that was equally intolerant of the views of the so-called unenlightened.

The study of religion highlights the imperfections and failures of Enlightenment norms. As the postmodern advocates of religious study point out, modern scientific methods themselves rely upon a set of scientifically unproveable assumptions and exclude other perspectives in ways akin to the parochial, tradition-bound outlook that the Enlightenment hoped to leave behind. Stated another way, the proponents of "scientific" models of study have no way of conducting a dialogue about truth or meaning with persons who refuse to accept the Enlightenment's own very parochial conception of knowledge.

This postmodern religious critique of the Enlightenment demonstrates the social character of learning and helps undermine the modern exaltation of the rational autonomous individual. Through its elevation of the Enlightenment ideal of objective science, the modern university has evolved into a body or community of scholarship that validates one kind of knowledge and excludes all others. Ironically, as the Jewish scholar Jon D. Levenson has argued, the Enlightenment account of knowledge is even more ruthlessly intolerant than religiously informed conceptions, because the latter by analogy can understand and appreciate rival systems of truth, even that embodied by the contemporary university. But the Enlightenment idea of truth, because rooted in the assumption that all other approaches are prejudiced and intolerant, can logically provide no space for alternative models.

These criticisms of the universities' neglect of religion have also generated assertions about the positive contribution that faith can make to a good education rightly conceived. Today's advocates of religion on campus argue that faith can supply the meaning or purpose that an undergraduate education so often lacks. In effect, religious perspectives provide faculty and students with the ability to ask the perennial questions and to see particular subjects as parts of a larger whole. This argument for including religion in higher education often includes a certain amount of hostility to the idea that believing scholars need to be accorded a seat at the academic table merely because intellectual or cultural diversity requires it. Including religion as an affirmation of the equality of all ideas and opinions ends up disemboweling faith of its own unified and coherent account of truth. Religion cannot be merely an area of study among many because it involves a quest to arrive at an integrated understanding of the cosmos. Rather than merely supplementing the current curriculum and its various academic specializations, faith should actually lead to a radical reform of higher education. The best texts, arguments, and scholarly practices should be used for the pursuit of a religiously informed understanding of the true, the good, and the beautiful. This argument for religion emphasizes its capacity to supply the integration and meaning that contemporary higher education lacks because of its overly narrow and fragmented specializations.

If these criticisms of the secular university sound familiar, the reason is that they are very similar to the complaints that led to the founding of religious studies departments in the first place. In fact, the parallels between today's debates about religion on campus and those of the post–World War II era are remarkable. Just two generations earlier, many faculty and administrators believed that the creation of religion departments in which students would explore perennial questions and learn about the importance of religion to Western civilization might supply a crucial spiritual, humanistic, pro-Western component to an educational system obsessed with scientific methodology. Religion departments would also provide a space in which faculty and students could form religious perspectives on the other academic disciplines. In effect, religion programs would help provide the meaning as well as form the humane values young adults needed in order to become liberally educated, responsible citizens.

But religious studies hardly proved to be the solution

that its advocates envisioned. The project failed, not because of faulty implementation but because of fundamental tensions between faith and modern learning. The moral to the history of religious studies is this: adding religion to the curriculum will not fix what ails American higher education.

Thus, to treat faith as yet another identity-defining characteristic along the lines of race or gender is to add to the already cacophonous character of the modern university and to deny that religion can form the educationally integrating purpose that its proponents desire. The idea that religion is similar to race or gender is rooted in a pluralistic model of higher education. In this model the academy brings together a collection of diverse individuals from different backgrounds and provides them neutral space within which they may politely disagree. Such a liberal and individualistic conception of advanced learning implicitly rejects the idea that higher education ought to be a shared intellectual endeavor governed by common convictions and standards.

The more astute advocates for religion in the university understand that faith has too often been promoted as a supplement and that a university truly hospitable to religion would require fundamental restructuring. Instead of merely adding a religion major here or more religion-oriented courses in the liberal arts curriculum there, a genuinely religion-directed academy would require a complete reassessment of higher education's purpose and function, with revised standards for teaching and research to match. The denominational colleges of the nineteenth century and the universities of medieval Europe serve as examples of alternative academic structures in which religion was woven into the purpose and execution of higher learning. But these historical precedents demonstrate how difficult the task of integrating religion into American higher education is, for they suggest models that have been rejected in favor of both the specialization and pragmatism that now dominate American colleges and universities. In other words, to study religion adequately and to have it inform the very premises of a liberal education would require a series of new institutions. Perhaps this is the path that those serious about religion should ultimately pursue; it is certainly the case that this road has already been taken by several colleges, such as Christendom and Patrick Henry in Virginia, Thomas More in New Hampshire, and New St. Andrews in Idaho. Even so, the need for different institutional forms confirms the point that religion is not a subject easily included in the current configuration and aims of the American university.

A PLAUSIBLE RATIONALE

We now know from whence the very idea of "religious studies" came, and we have some reason to believe that it cannot fulfill the role that religious believers had once hoped it could. But if that is the case, why study religion? Despite all the problems with the discipline we have outlined thus far, this question still allows a number of answers. For the student who practices a faith, it is possible that the study of religion may be an aid to devotion—particularly at denominationally orthodox schools, but even at public and secular private institutions, as long as one enters religious studies knowing what one is likely to encounter.

Many students enroll in a course on religion to learn more about a particular faith and in the hope that the instruction they receive will confirm or deepen an already existing religious conviction. In a similar vein, other students may hope to expose a perplexed or searching conscience to a possible source of spiritual hope and meaning. As sensible as these motivations for studying religion may be, it is important for students to realize that such impulses will often be frustrated in the contemporary academy.

Take the following case. Say a student from a Lutheran family and church goes off to a highly selective liberal arts college. She is a German major but knows her college has a religion major and decides to review the catalogue for courses related to her religious upbringing. She sees a course on the Protestant Reformation and believes it will give her the opportunity to study the German Reformer, Martin Luther, in some depth. She attends the first class and comes away seriously disappointed. The professor's goal is not to demonstrate the plausibility of Luther's (or any of his fellow Protestants') views but to show how the Reformers were creatures of a specific time with ideas now superseded by the march of history. Thus, rather than finding a course that might help her reach a deeper understanding and appreciation of Lutheran teachings and practices, this young woman has encountered a different kind of instruction. The professor may explain why Luther taught certain doctrines but not why those teachings are valuable or even true.

This illustration is instructive on several levels. The first concerns the difference between the academy and other institutions responsible for religious instruction. Students must keep in mind that the church, synagogue, and family are the best places to receive the kind of teaching that encourages and deepens faith. If students sign up for courses in religion expecting the same kind of teaching they might receive at home or at church, then they have overestimated American higher education and missed the importance of disparate agencies of religious tutelage. On another level, the example of this student reveals the uniqueness of religious faith and how it differs from the other minority identities to which it is often likened. However reductionistic it may be to speak of a gendered, racial, or sexual perspective, the categories of race, gender and sexual orientation differ essentially from faith. The former emerge naturally from the reality of human embodiment. Faith, in contrast, is something supernatural, something that has a divine source—so the historic Western religions have always taught. Because faith is unique, not something understood readily by the nonbeliever, to take a course in religion at an institution that does not require a religious commitment from its faculty with the expectation that it will deepen one's faith is to engage in a confusion of categories. This is why the Old and New Testaments constantly refer to the faithful as being different from the rest of the world.

At the other end of the spectrum, some students take courses in religion from the perspective of critical distance or objective detachment. The view that religion should be studied in a questioning manner, with a measure of skepticism about its claims, continues to be a common one in the American academy. In fact, the three great modern debunkers of religion—Karl Marx, Friedrich Nietzsche, and Sigmund Freud—still implicitly inform the perspectives of many faculty. At its most extreme, then, this approach to religion examines faith as something that prevents people from grasping the real nature of things. The obvious difficulty for students of faith taking courses in religion is that such study often ends up undermining the faith they received at home. Sometimes faculty members can even be aggressive about raising doubts among their students. In other cases, they may stand closer to the liberal wing of a theological tradition and so ask questions and present ideas that students from conservative backgrounds find troubling. Of course, some professors believe that the best way to treat religion is the way one usually considers any other human subject, with sympathy and tolerance.

To illustrate how the critical study of religion poses a dilemma for students interested in learning more about their own faiths, consider again the case of the Lutheran student mentioned earlier. In the course on the Protestant Reformation, she has encountered a method of study that is largely historical, tracing the ideas of early Protestants to earlier theological developments and also revealing the degree to which European politics shaped different aspects of the Reformers' ideas and endeavors. The overriding impression is that these religious leaders, whom the student was predisposed to consider heroic in character and judgment, were limited in their accomplishments because they were bound by the peculiar circumstances of their location and era. But if students remember that the best place to look for religious encouragement is not in the classroom but in nonacademic settings committed to encouraging devoted learning, they may also appropriate important lessons imparted by critical approaches to religion. In fact, the study of religion benefits from both approaches, from an investigation of both the temporal factors shaping belief and the matters of eternal consequence that also drive religious traditions. Students in search of greater wisdom and religious encouragement can profit from the critical study of religion, then, precisely because it leads to the deeper understanding that faith is not a disembodied set of aspirations or ideals but rather takes shape within the mysterious complexity of human existence.

Still, there is one reason for studying religion that applies to believers and nonbelievers alike, one that we have already mentioned, namely, that to understand the history and teachings of the Jewish and Christian traditions is to understand better Western civilization and culture and, ultimately, oneself.[2]

This justification for the study of religion is an improvement over the earlier mid-twentieth-century rationale for the academic study of religion advanced by various Protestants because it permits a multiplicity of approaches and answers. Perhaps the biggest strike against the initial argument for the inclusion of religion as an academic discipline was the way it privileged Protestantism to the exclusion of other religions. This, of course, can no longer be the case. For obvious historical reasons, the study of religion in the West would clearly give more attention to Christianity than to other world religions. But such a concentration need not imply the superiority of the Christian religion, nor need it condone Christian cultural hegemony, Protestant or otherwise, as a surreptitious goal.

Another problem with the original configuration of

religious studies in American learning was its failure to carve out a subject matter or scholarly method that clearly distinguished it from other fields. Religion departments were, in effect, arrangements of convenience, places in which to put Protestant academics, whose teaching would stem the tide of secularism and relativism in the university and society at large. But even during the middle decades of the twentieth century religion departments were not the only places where students could find courses on faith. One of the best examples was Harvard University's program in American Civilization, where Perry Miller, the great scholar of Puritanism, taught. During that era, undergraduates at Harvard could likely learn more Protestant divinity in a classroom with Miller than with any of the faculty at the nearby Harvard Divinity School. Consequently, an approach to religion that begins with the question of its influence on the West has the advantage of engaging the range of academic disciplines covering Western culture and in which the subject of faith naturally arises. Instead of looking exclusively for courses offered in religion departments, students may very well discover important classes on religious subjects and themes in history, literature, philosophy, art history, and political science departments.

An additional benefit is that the study of religion's contribution to the West does not assume that such influence has been for good or ill but instead leaves open the question of when and where faith has functioned as a beneficial or detrimental aspect of Western society. As such, this approach has the potential for being more evenhanded than was religious studies as originally conceived, when the assumption prevailed that religious influences on the West were invariably positive and welcome. The regard for religion in any particular course will vary from professor to professor. Even so, because of the complicated history behind the academic discipline of religious studies, and in particular because of a lingering sense of shame in many religion departments over the field's initial partiality to Protestantism, students may discover that Christianity receives a fairer treatment from faculty outside religious studies than from those within the field.

Besides having uncritically embraced a selective, overtly Protestant narrative of the West's triumph, the religious studies' field as it developed in the middle of the twentieth century also made other mistakes. For one, it viewed the West (and hence Protestant Christianity) as synonymous with modernity and its particular conceptions of freedom and democracy that emphasized individual autonomy. It also obscured the important discontinuities that often exist between religion and culture. In other words, the study of religion so closely identified church and culture in the development of the West that "faith" in, say, American freedom and democracy (a form of civil religion) could easily be conflated with faith in the God who is supposed to transcend nations and politics. The study of the Judaic and Christian religions' influence on the history and culture of the West, then, needs to be an endeavor that is open to both critics and defenders of faith. It ought not to assume that religion has always been a wholesome contribution, nor should it simply be a vehicle for demonstrating faith's pernicious hold upon the mind of the West. But in the current academic climate, and in the light of religious studies' difficult past, simply keeping such questions open is arguably the best remaining basis for exploring religion in the modern academy. Indeed, the presumptions encountered, even in negative estimates of faith's influence on the West, may for religious believers generate greater insight into the exact claims and practices of their particular faith traditions.

Returning to our Lutheran student in search of her own heritage, the study of religion in the West's development will not necessarily satisfy her personal reasons for looking for courses on religion. But what the cultural approach yields is a good chance that this student will actually find lectures, readings and courses on the subject in which she is interested. In fact, students who wish to study religious questions and themes will readily find that even if a history, philosophy, or literature course does not mention religion in the catalogue description, they may well be able to write a research paper on religious themes that inevitably arise from the course's material. Consequently, even if the study of religion appears to be merely a supplement, and an inferior one at that, to the cultural heritage of the West, it does provide a forum for the exploration of religion in ways more beneficial than any tried in the past or currently proposed. It is not without its own weaknesses and difficulties. But in the current academic climate, and in the light of religious studies' difficult past, it is arguably the best basis for exploring the influence of the most important religious thinkers and texts upon the West.

III. RELIGION IN THE WEST

BEFORE THE CHRISTIAN EMPIRE

The most obvious place to begin to understand the influence of religion in the West is with the Jewish and Christian scriptures. The canonical books for Jews, Roman Catholics, and Protestants differ in important ways. For Jews, the Hebrew Bible consists of those writings—the Law, the Prophets, and Wisdom Literature—that Christians designate as the Old Testament. In the Jewish tradition the Hebrew Bible is part of a larger body of literature, including the Talmud, Midrash, and rabbinical commentaries, that constitutes the source of religious authority for Judaism. The Christian Bible includes the Old and New Testaments, the latter including the Gospels and Epistles. Where Protestant and Roman Catholic scriptures differ is with a body of writings known as the Apocrypha. This material was translated into Greek along with the Hebrew Bible as part of the Septuagint (the Greek version of the Old Testament), but the Apocryphal writings were clearly distinct from the Law, Prophets, and Wisdom writings. Roman Catholics include the Apocrypha in their Bibles, Protestants do not.

Most religion departments will offer courses in the Jewish and Christian scriptures, though they will not necessarily distinguish among the different configurations of canonical materials. Jewish studies programs generally will also provide instruction in the Hebrew Bible, while at some institutions the department of Ancient Near Eastern Studies has become the clearinghouse for courses on biblical literature. It is also usually possible to find classes on the Bible in other departments. Political philosophers and ethicists will sometimes use scripture as the basis for reflecting on important questions in these fields. Historians and literature faculty may examine the Bible's influence on a national or regional culture. They may also read the Bible as a form of literature, or even study popular biblical figures—such as Abraham, Moses, David, Jesus, or Mary—as cultural icons. For the devout student, some of these approaches to the biblical writings may seem tangential at best, irreverent at worst. Still, as part of understanding the influence of the Bible on Western society, such courses have merit. Indeed, an awareness of the major themes, genres, and stories of the Hebrew and Christian scriptures is crucial to understanding religion's role in forming the mind of the West, since these writings have functioned as nor-

mative not only for Jewish and Christian faith and practice but also for Western civilization generally.

The immense impact of the Bible on Western culture
is the result, at least in part, of the unexpected appeal of
Christianity to a powerful ruler. As much as church apolo-
gists might attribute Christianity's role in shaping Western
society to the general appeal of church teaching, Emperor
Constantine's conversion in 312 and his subsequent decision to make Christianity the official religion of the Roman empire granted the church a place of prominence in
the ensuing development of the West that would not dissi-
pate substantially until the revolutions of the late eighteenth
century. Some of the earliest ecumenical creeds, such as
the Nicene (325) and the Chalcedonian (451), which established the precise formulation of trinitarian orthodoxy, were
the result of councils of bishops assembled at the call of
the emperor, who in turn enforced these teachings as part
of the state's religion. Even the compilation of those writings to be included in the Christian scriptures, a process
that had taken shape in informal ways since the late first
century, became official activities between the fourth and
eighth centuries through the process of convening church
councils, most of which required the consent of the em-

peror. The church's influence on society could not have been as extensive as it was without the state's recognition and enforcement of the Christian religion as the imperial norm.

Finding courses on the teachings of the ecumenical creeds and the politics that lay behind them will likely be difficult. It may require extensive searching in the syllabi of classes on ancient history or, with luck, taking a course on early Christianity in a religion department or divinity school. But the creeds that these councils produced, along with subsequent official formulations by religious bodies in their creedal statements and catechisms, are crucial to understanding the precise content and scope of a particular church's teachings and practices. In fact, an important consideration for studying Western Christianity is that creeds and catechisms are a much more reliable index to the nature of Christian belief than are the ideas and opinions of individual believers. The latter usually have no official standing and so do not qualify as authoritative teachings, while the former generally reflect a deliberative process conducted by church officials and intended to establish boundaries for both ordination and the instruction and inclusion of members.

As valuable as ecclesiastical councils and creeds and catechisms may be, the writings of individual Christian teachers and theologians have also been decisive in the interpretation of religion's place in Western society. Eusebius of Caesarea (260–341), although an Eastern church leader, is significant because of his work as a historian and apologist in the new environment that was created by Christianity's status as the empire's official religion. His *Ecclesiastical History* and *Life of Constantine* were particularly revealing of the ways in which Christianity could be accommodated for the purposes of public life. Eusebius had a variety of aims in writing the history of the church in the manner he did, some of which reflected his own position in the theological controversies that had led Constantine to call the Council of Nicea. But one central theme in Eusebius's historical writings is a conception of divine providence in which he interprets Constantine's conversion and recognition of the church as a crucial development in its success and prosperity. For Eusebius, the emergence of Christianity as the faith of the empire is the culmination of salvation history. In turn, he treats the rule of Constantine as the fulfillment of divine promise, thus identifying political rule with divine will. The emperor's function as the head of the church would be a feature that distinguished the Eastern church from its Western counterpart, a distinction not fully realized until the break between the Eastern (Orthodox) and Western (Roman Catholic) churches in 1054. By making Christianity the established religion of the empire, Constantine, along with Eusebius's justification of his action, created a tension with which Christians have had to deal since the fourth century—namely, the degree to which church affairs and civil society are or ought to be separate, and, by extension, whether the emperor or the bishop is the ultimate authority in the ecclesiastical realm.

Part of what makes Augustine of Hippo (354–430) worthy of study are his own struggles with this question. One of the West's most insightful and fruitful minds, Augustine's moving account of his conversion to Christianity in *The Confessions* (400) has served as an important text for modern interpretations of the formation of the self. But perhaps of more lasting consequence has been his consideration of the significance of Rome's fall (410) for the history of the church and Western civilization. In *The City of God*, begun in 413 and not completed until thirteen years later, the North African bishop developed the idea of "two

cities," the city of man and the city of God. Contrary both
to imperial theologians like Eusebius, who saw the hand of
the divine in the political history of civilizations, and to

Even if courses on the Bible's origins or the formulation of its ecumenical creeds, or on the early church's leaders, or on the religious components of imperial politics are difficult to find, books on these subjects are
not. On the development of the Christian scriptures, Hans Von
Campenhausen's *The Formation of the Christian Bible* (London, 1972)
is still a reliable and informative guide. A more recent treatment, one
that unnecessarily emphasizes the diversity of early Christianity but still
provides assistance to the recent scholarship on the Bible's formation, is
Bart D. Ehrman's *Lost Christianities: The Battle for Scripture and the
Faiths We Never Knew* (New York, 1993). The eminent historical
theologian Jaroslav Pelikan's *Whose Bible Is It? A History of the Scriptures
through the Ages* (New York, 2005) is another important book on this
subject. Interpretations of the Bible will invariably depend upon the
religious identity of the interpreter. Ronald Knox's *A Commentary on
the Gospels* (London, 1952) represents an insightful Roman Catholic
perspective. Brevard S. Child's *Biblical Theology of the Old and New
Testaments: Theological Reflection on the Christian Bible* (Minneapolis,
1993) offers the same for Protestants. In addition, Leon Kass, though
not trained as a biblical interpreter, discovers within the first book of the
Hebrew scriptures a source not only of Jewish wisdom and ethical
reflection but also of profound insight into the human condition; see
his *Beginning of Wisdom: Reading Genesis* (New York, 2003). Other
worthwhile books on the Bible include Adam Nicholson's *God's Secre-
taries: The Making of the King James Bible* (San Francisco, 2003) and
David Daniell's *The Bible in English: Its History and Influence* (New
York, 2003), which examine the influence of English translations of the
Bible on English literature, and Robert Alter's *The Art of Biblical
Narrative* (New York, 1983), which examines the significance of the
Bible's (primarily the Old Testament's) literary structure.

the church's opponents who blamed Rome's fall on Christianity, Augustine avoided either demonizing or divinizing the political realm. The city of God is that polity where true piety rules and is distinct from the city of man, where

---

Although not directly concerned with the formation and interpretation of the canonical scriptures, the work of Robert Louis Wilken, especially in such books as *The Spirit of Early Christian Thought: Seeking the Face of God* (New Haven, CT, 2003), yields a highly instructive and richly textured account of the lives of the first Christians. J. N. D. Kelly's *Early Christian Doctrines* (London, 1958) is still the classic treatment of the ideas and arguments that informed the debates which generated the first Christian creeds. More recently, Pelikan has produced a reference work of epic proportions that covers in four volumes not only the first Christian creeds but also all subsequent formal creedal declarations: *Creeds and Confessions of the Christian Faith* (New Haven, CT, 2003). The companion volume to this massive undertaking, Pelikan's *Credo: Historical and Theological Guide to the Creeds and Confessions of Faith in the Christian Tradition* (New Haven, CT, 2003), offers astute insight into the development of Christian thought from the earliest creeds to the present. The emergence of Christianity as the religion of the empire is a vast topic that receives perceptive treatment in Ramsey MacMullen's *Christianizing the Roman Empire* (New Haven, CT, 1986). An older version of the subject on a grand scale comes from the great nineteenth-century historian Jacob Burckhardt in *The Age of Constantine the Great* (trans.; London, 1949). Constantine's biographer and bishop, Eusebius, has not yet received close critical inspection, but Timothy Barnes's *Constantine and Eusebius* (Cambridge, 1984), is a careful account of Christianity's emergence as the official religion of the empire that proceeds through an examination of these men's lives. The unsurpassed study of Augustine remains Peter Brown's *Augustine of Hippo: A Biography* (London, 1967).

civil law and imperial authority govern. These cities were not necessarily at odds, but neither could they be identified with one another as Eusebius had believed. Augustine did not abandon the high view of divine providence that was espoused by imperial theologians. He argued that God still controlled the affairs of Rome and its civilization even in the midst of adversity. At the same time, he advised that Christian virtues were clearly advantageous to the prosperity of the city of man. But whatever peace and prosperity the empire displayed, he added, were only types or foreshadowings of the heavenly city, whose vindication awaited the end of human history. By distinguishing the ultimate ends of religion from the temporal ones of empire, Augustine set the terms that would allow future Christians, and others, to navigate the tension between religious and political authority created by Constantine's conversion.

THE RISE OF CHRISTENDOM

With the fall of Rome and the decline of an imperial presence in the West, the Roman Catholic Church became the chief mechanism for providing social stability and preserving the cultural and intellectual inheritance of classical antiquity. The papacy itself possessed political and cultural significance by virtue of its location in Rome, which was not only the capital of the Western branch of the empire, but was also the only Western city of the ancient church's patriarchates (equivalent, in effect, to archbishoprics of the largest dioceses), which also included Jerusalem, Constantinople, Alexandria, and Antioch. During the first half millennium of the Middle Ages (500–1000), the papacy commanded the allegiance of Western Christians but lacked organizational structures to make its recognized supremacy felt. This situation changed with the Gregorian reform movement of the eleventh century. First with Pope Leo IX (1048–54) and then with Gregory VII (1073–85), the papacy emerged in the West as the center of religious life through forming a tightly organized church and elaborate system of canon law. This reform movement was designed to recover the truly spiritual vocation of ecclesiastical office. But it had important consequences for political and cultural life in the West, since these popes began to assert, with greater force, the papacy's preeminent position of a divinely ordained and hierarchical Christian society. One specific expression of the church's ecclesiastical authority was its rejection of the investiture of bishops (i.e., their selection and confirmation) by secular rulers, an implicit rebuke to the prince's role in church affairs, a Constantinian inheritance. Ironically, the assertion of the papacy's spiritual prerogatives produced a massive administrative and legal system that in the later Middle Ages made the church the most powerful political institution in the West. The increased power of the papacy also finally severed the weakening ties between the churches of the East and West. Debates in the eleventh century concerning the phrasing of the Nicene Creed (especially its "filioque" clause, which asserts that the Holy Spirit "proceeds from the Father and the Son" rather than the Father alone, the formulation insisted on by the Eastern church) led the papacy to maintain its universal sovereignty in ways that ended in 1054 when officials from both the Eastern and Western churches excommunicated each other.

During this period, the church also revived Western intellectual life through the unlikely agency of monasticism. The legacy of specific expressions of Christian devotion in Egypt and Syria, the emergene of monastic communities dedicated to personal holiness and charitable service in the sixth century became a common feature of Western Christianity through the Rule (i.e., way or system) of Saint Benedict. Over time, the monastic orders provided the resources for the West's intellectual life by functioning as centers where the church' most important thinkers produced their work. These orders also retained a near monopoly on book production until the late Middle Ages. In effect, the monastic ideal of withdrawal from the world in order to cultivate virtue overlapped with the kind of retreat necessary for contemplation and reflection. Consequently the monasteries emerged as nurseries for the life of the mind. It took the rise of the university in such cities as Bologna, Oxford, and Paris for the intellectual preeminence of the cloister to begin to diminish. And even these new academic institutions were designed specifically for the training of secular clergy, thus extending the West's dependence on the church for the nurturance of its greatest intellectual and cultural achievements.

No figure better illustrates the church's impact on Western thought than Thomas Aquinas (1225–74). Born in Italy and trained from the age of six by monks at the Benedictine abbey of Monte Cassino, Aquinas eventually joined the newly formed Dominican order of friars after studying at the University of Naples. His most prominent academic appointment was at the University of Paris, where he taught for more than a decade. Throughout his life he also taught at various schools in his native land and wrote extensively. Aquinas is the foremost theologian of the Middle Ages, and his writings have exerted a prodigious influence on Roman Catholicism to the present day. His publications are also important for revealing the character of the intellectual life in the West during the so-called cultural renaissance of the twelfth and thirteenth centuries. Aquinas was an especially gifted practitioner of the scholastic method, a highly systematic way of reading authoritative texts. This academic program united scholars in the Western universities down to the seventeenth century and so established Aquinas's influence.

————————

Courses on Christianity in the medieval period will most likely be found in history programs large enough to support professors working in that era, though at Roman Catholic universities and colleges medieval studies often occupy a substantial part of the curriculum. Some religion departments will offer classes on Aquinas, while English majors will find outlets for exploring the Middle Ages in courses on Beowolf and Chaucer. Many philosophers keep alive the study of Aquinas, who with Aristotle is considered a progenitor of "natural law" philosophy, and will teach an occasional course or seminar on his thought. These classes may include more general considerations of medieval philosophy, as well. Students of political philosophy may also discover courses on the politics of Christendom that delve into disputes between emperor and pope. And, of course, where courses are unavailable, books abound. Important general works on the influence of Christianity on Western society and culture include:

Aquinas is even more significant because he carefully synthesized Western Christian reflection with the writings of Greek antiquity. An ironic twist in the Western church's efforts to restore Christianity in the Holy Lands during the Crusades of the eleventh century had been that it renewed the West's acquaintance with the all-but-forgotten Greek philosophers, thinkers that the Arab-Muslim world had already rehabilitated and used to make great advances in math and science. Aristotle was the most prominent figure to be resurrected in the West, particularly his works on logic, metaphysics, and natural science. Aquinas made use of newly available translations of Aristotle and wrote sev-

---

Christopher Dawson, *Religion and the Rise of Western Culture* (New York, 1950), R. W. Southern, *Western Society and the Church in the Middle Ages* (London, 1970), and Norman F. Cantor, *The Civilization of the Middle Ages* (New York, 1993). For gaining a good grasp of the history behind and emergence of the papacy as an institution of unparalleled influence in the medieval West, Walter Ullmann's *A Short History of the Papacy in the Middle Ages* (London, 1972) is a good place to start. The political controversies that developed in the West as the result of the rival claims of pope and emperor, debates that shaped Western politics profoundly, receive valuable treatment in Brian Tierney's, *The Crisis of Church and State, 1050–1300* (Englewood Cliffs, NJ, 1964). More comprehensive in scope and magisterial in interpretation is Ernst Kantorowicz's *The King's Two Bodies* (Princeton, NJ, 1957), which explores the intricacies of medieval political theology and their importance for the West.

eral commentaries on the Greek thinker. In addition he employed significant elements of Aristotelian thought in his own formulation and defense of Christianity. Of course, Aquinas also drew heavily on previous Western theologians in articulating Christian doctrine. Still, in his thought and career several strands of the West's cultural development run together: the legacy of monasticism in preserving intellectual life, the academic renaissance of the high Middle Ages, and the West's rediscovery of Aristotle. As a preeminent figure in each of these developments, Aquinas's stature in the premodern West is second only to Augustine's.

Western Christendom Divided

The medieval synthesis exemplified in scholastic theology and the first European universities began to unravel in the

---

Students interested in the rise of universities and the character of medieval learning would be well advised to turn to Charles Homer Haskins's *The Renaissance of the Twelfth Century* (Cambridge, MA, 1979), a book covering the vigorous intellectual and cultural life that shaped the great medieval universities. The collection of essays in *Universities in the Middle Ages,* volume one of *A History of the University in Europe*, edited by Hilde de Ridder-Symoens and Walter Roegg (Cambridge, 2003), is more technical, but also demonstrates the church's role in the origins of the West's institutions of learning. For a better understanding of medieval philosophy, Josef Pieper's *Scholasticism: Personalities and Problems of Medieval Philosophy* (New

sixteenth century, thanks largely to the rise of Protestantism. The religious significance of the Protestant Reformation is best grasped through the writings of its most important figures, foremost among whom stands Martin Luther (1483–1546), the first Protestant to challenge successfully the authority of the papacy. The son of a copper miner, Luther entered the priesthood at the age of twenty-four and began to study theology. This task eventually took him to the monastery and university in the Saxony city of Wittenberg. His theological inquiry was bound up deeply with his own personal doubts and spiritual struggles, and as he resolved these dilemmas his calls for reforming the Roman Catholic Church became more urgent. Luther urged the church to make both organizational and theological changes, from greater autonomy for local bishops

---

York, 1960) and Etienne Gilson's *The Spirit of Medieval Philosophy* (London, 1936) are sources of wisdom. The best place to inquire about Aquinas is by reading the man himself, his multivolume *Summa Theologiae* representing the best expression of his thought. But because his scholastic style is often off-putting to moderns, secondary works may provide a more accessible way to approach the great medieval theologian. G. K. Chesterton's biography, *St. Thomas Aquinas: The Dumb Ox* (London, 1933) is an engaging and faithful account, while Etienne Gilson's *The Christian Philosophy of St. Thomas Aquinas* (London, 1957) is a careful and systematic treatment of Aquinas's thought.

from Rome, to an understanding of salvation that stressed faith over works as the means of becoming righteous.

Luther was not systematic in his thought, but he was certainly prolific. An English translation of his published works runs to fifty-five volumes and includes all manner of writings, from the occasional treatises in which he justified his break with Rome to commentaries on specific biblical books. Perhaps even more important to the spread of Protestantism was Luther's translation of the Bible into German, an endeavor that set the pattern for other Protestant denominations, which typically strove to ensure that Christianity's foundational text was accessible to the average believer. Arguably the most influential of Luther's essays were "Two Kinds of Righteousness" (1519), "The Freedom of a Christian" (1520), and "The Pagan Servitude of the Church" (1520). In these treatises, formulated during debates with Roman Catholic authorities, the major themes of Luther's theology emerged.

After Luther, the Protestant Reformer of greatest stature was John Calvin (1509–64). A Frenchman who had grown up just outside Paris in the home of a church jurist, Calvin was trained in theology and law. His conversion as a young man to the new Protestant movement eventually landed him in the city-republic of Geneva, where he would pastor the French-speaking Swiss and French Protestant exiles for the rest of his life, with the exception of a brief period in Strasbourg. Whereas Luther's writings were occasional, Calvin's exuded systematic exactness. His two monumental literary efforts were *The Institutes of the Christian Religion*, first written in 1536 but revised several times until its last edition in 1559, and his commentaries on the Bible, written over the course of his life as part of his regular teaching duties in the Genevan church. Unlike Luther, whose writing sometimes ran afoul of the requirements of intellectual consistency, Calvin was relentlessly logical. And it is to this faculty that many historians have attributed the Calvinistic doctrines of predestination and original sin. Having been trained in the literary studies of Renaissance humanism, Calvin was also a sensitive interpreter of the Bible, which he read in its original languages of Hebrew and Greek.

The efforts of Luther and Calvin gave birth respectively to the Lutheran and Reformed branches of the Protestant movement. The other major Protestant churchly tradition to come out of the sixteenth century was Anglicanism. From the time that Luther's writings first gained currency in England during the 1520s to 1550s, when Calvin's influence made itself felt through the English refugees returning from Geneva, the Church of England rose and fell according to the fortunes of the Tudor monarchy. What particularly aggravated the situation and gave Protestantism a political foothold was King Henry VIII's inability to produce a male heir, which involved a succession of wives and the need to have marriages to former wives annulled. When the papacy refused to grant Henry's request, in 1534 he declared himself the head of the Church of England.

The Church of England's confession of faith in *The Thirty-Nine Articles* dates from a period when Calvinists were in ascendancy. Even so, because of the need for political stability during the reign of Elizabeth I, attempts to implement Calvinistic reforms as consistently as had happened in Geneva and Scotland encountered fierce opposition. This inability to carry forward reforms in the Church of England spawned a movement often referred to as Puritanism. Frustrations with the religious and ecclesiastical situation in England would eventually prompt a considerable group of Puritans to migrate to the New World, where they founded the Massachusetts Bay Colony.

As the example of the Church of England indicates, the success, and sometimes the failure, of the Protestant Reformation was bound up with the affairs of statecraft. Furthermore, Protestantism's political dimensions were crucial to the undoing of the West's ideal of a unified cultural life bound together by a common faith. For this reason, the division of Western Christianity marks an extremely important episode in the West's history and its culture. Since the sixteenth century, the West has been haunted by several grave and interrelated questions. Without a shared religion, is there an adequate foundation for the public or civic flourishing of the true, the good, and the beautiful? What is the proper role for religion in society, especially if it is a source of division? Is it possible, or even desirable, to restore the cultural unity that once prevailed in Western Europe, and if so how should such a restoration be attempted? These problems have animated the reflections of leading philosophers, poets, and politicians in modern Western history and they continue to be objects of study in a variety of courses in the humanities and social sciences. Even in those sectors of the academy where the agenda appears to be radically multicultural, the social and political changes mobilized by the sixteenth century's religious history are implicitly the basis of calls for greater diversity and equality, since it is believed that the cultural uniformity which formerly prevailed was responsible for enormous oppression and intolerance.

The polemics fanned into flame by the Protestant Reformation were not simply occasions for Protestants and Roman Catholics to dispute each other. The debates and arguments also enlisted one Protestant church against another. As much as the modern temper may recoil from doctrinal disputes, the theological climate created by religious division actually expanded vastly the theological resources of Protestants and Roman Catholics alike. Heightened self-awareness among Lutherans, Reformed, Anglicans, and Roman Catholics resulted in academic theological treatises and disputations that rivaled the scholastic theology of the Middle Ages. Some of the greatest accomplishments of church councils during the early modern period were the fruit of this jealousy for a particular theological tradition. The Council of Trent for Roman Catholics (1540s to 1560s), the Book of Concord for Lutherans (1577), and the Westminster Assembly (1640s) for Presbyterians are examples of ecclesiastical assemblies that met to deliberate on the new religious teachings and to craft appropriate responses. The creeds, catechisms, and canons written by these councils are a rich source for understanding both foundational matters in modern Roman Catholic and Protestant identities and the issues that divided the soul of the West.

Within the different churches, theologians rose to prominence because of their ability to defend their own doctrinal tradition and expose the weaknesses of others. For Roman Catholics, Cardinal Robert Bellarmine (1542–1621) proved the ablest apologist of the early modern era, devoting most of his attention to issues of papal authority. Within Anglican circles, Richard Hooker (1554–1600) elaborated the principles of church order in his *Of the Laws of Ecclesiastical Polity* (1593), which would set the Church of England on a middle course between Rome, Wittenberg, and Geneva and consolidate Queen Elizabeth I's title as head of the Anglican communion. Johann Gerhard (1582–1673), whose work defended the creeds of the Lutheran churches, was the greatest of his confession's theologians during this era. For Reformed Protestants, Francis Turretin (1623–87) defended and expounded Calvin's teachings in ways that were influential well beyond Geneva. Each of these theologians provides both an example of the doctrinal polemics of the late sixteenth and early seventeenth centuries and of the orthodoxy that defined their respective traditions.

Because religion was still of vital interest to the state—the legacy of Constantine was indeed a long and complicated one—the sort of differences articulated by Roman Catholic and Protestant theologians and councils had enormous political repercussions. The most woeful example of political division caused by theological disunity was the Thirty Years War, a series of battles that ravaged northern European society between 1618 and 1648. The war's sources were twofold. First, it reflected the Holy Roman Empire's decline and its inability still to sustain social and political cohesion. Second, the empire's loss of control was tied to the religious divisions that attended the fracturing of Western Christianity at the time of the Protestant Reformation. The actual narrative of the war and its political implications are complicated and not easily summarized. But its religious and cultural significance are not. The Thirty Years War was an example of religious warfare at its worst, and its memory permanently scarred the West's conscience. Even though Roman Catholic and Protestant churches would continue to be part of the political establishment after the Peace of Westphalia of 1648, with territories designated according to their confessional majority, the war became proof of the dangerous alchemy involved in mixing religious conviction and statecraft.

The resulting tension between church and crown was crucial to the construction of modern ideas of the state. Seventeenth-century political philosophers, such as John Locke (1632–1704) and Thomas Hobbes (1588–1679), haunted by the English Civil War of the 1640s, sought a basis other than faith for social order and the rule of law. The political antagonisms caused by religious division were by no means the only reason for those experiments in modern political philosophy which sought "natural" and "rational" sources for the principles of statecraft and institutions of civil society. But the philosophers' appeals to the state of nature, social contracts, and reason certainly stemmed partly from the problems posed by societies founded on religious ideals which now lacked religious uniformity. Although these developments in political philosophy represented a secular turn in reflection on the state, the thinkers themselves continued to contemplate human nature in ways that typically drew on Christian teaching about man's moral constitution. As such, studies in the history of political philosophy invite serious attention to religious themes and ideas.

CHRISTIANITY AND MODERNITY

After the American and French revolutions, religion in the West took on a markedly different character. The reasons for this were more than political. Economic, demographic, and scientific developments also challenged the religious status quo. In particular, the Enlightenment's quest for certainty through the exercise of human reason and the meth-

---

Courses on the early-modern period should be easy to find, and a university's offerings in political philosophy, history, literature, and religious studies should provide plenty of opportunity for students interested in exploring the religious dimensions of the momentous changes that took place in Europe during this time. Though somewhat dated, Roland H. Bainton's *Here I Stand: A Life of Martin Luther* (New York, 1955) is still the most accessible biography of the German reformer. On the social significance of Luther's ideas, A. G. Dickens's *German Nation and Martin Luther* (London, 1974) is a worthwhile study. OnCalvin, François Wendel's *Calvin: The Origins and Development of his Religious Thought* (London, 1963) remains a reliable guide. In addition, John T. McNeill's *History and Character of Calvinism* (New York, 1954) provides an impressive overview of the French Protestant's religious and cultural legacy. The history of the Church of England and its struggles with Puritanism is a complicated subject, but the essays collected in *The Study of Anglicanism*, edited by Stephen Sykes, John Booty, and Jonathan Knight (Minneapolis, 1998), along with Alan Simpson's *Puritanism in Old and New*

ods of modern science often became the basis for alleging the backwardness of faith. Combined with the social up- heaval provoked first by the sixteenth-century division of Western Christianity and followed by the religious wars of the seventeenth century, religion was doomed to lose its esteemed place in public life. Without the blessing of prince or emperor, faith needed other settings, more private ones, in order to flourish. And even in those cases where churches remained part of the cultural establishment, the difficulty of employing faith for social cohesion in religiously mixed

---

England (Chicago, 1959), should help students make some sense of Anglican complexities.

The ramifications of the division within Western Christianity are discussed ably from a Roman Catholic perspective in Christopher Dawson's *The Dividing of Christendom* (New York, 1965). Studies of the religious polemics emerging from the sixteenth century are not readily identified but two books that give a flavor of the issues to surface among Protestants and Catholics after the Reformation are John W. O'Malley's *Trent and All That: Renaming Catholicism in the Early Modern Era* (Cambridge, MA, 2002) and Philip Benedict's *Christ's Churches Purely Reformed: A Social History of Calvinism* (New Haven, CT, 2002).

On the various councils and creeds of the Reformation era, Pelikan's *Creeds and Confessions of the Christian Faith*, mentioned earlier, is the place to look. On the consequences of Western Christianity's division for political philosophy, Pierre Manent's *An Intellectual History of Liberalism* (Princeton, NJ, 1996) is concise yet profound.

settings prompted church leaders to look for new ways to nurture religious conviction. If in the premodern West, religion had been public (being part of the political establishment) and formal (involving external or outward manifestations of its legitimacy), religion in the modern West became private and informal.

The most obvious example of this shift was the burst of religious awakenings that developed within Anglo-American eighteenth-century Protestantism. At roughly the same time, and fairly independent of each other, John Wesley (1703–91) and Jonathan Edwards (1703–58) reevaluated older establishmentarian notions about faith and church life and developed new expressions of piety, often called "evangelical," to match Christianity's altered context. A priest in the Church of England, Wesley promoted an experiential and informal faith, often in settings where the religious establishment was nonexistent. Although he wrote extensively on various aspects of Christianity and the church's responsibilities, Wesley's greatest contribution was to create structures—both individual and associational—for this new form of devotion. The label applied to Wesley's efforts was "Methodism," even though he remained in the Church of England until his death. Whereas

Wesley was the organizer, Edwards was the philosopher of evangelical religion. He wrote extensive treatises on why the new emphasis on personal experience was legitimate, while also promoting the "heart religion" he defended through his own work as a Congregationalist minister.

This revival of religious earnestness in Old and New England was united by the remarkable career of George Whitefield (1714–70). A younger associate of Wesley's and a priest of the Church of England, Whitefield preached extensively throughout Great Britain and North America during his lifetime. The revivals he led became legendary throughout the English-speaking world and even in parts of Protestant Europe. The net effect of his and other revivalists' efforts was to introduce a new kind of Protestant devotion. No longer geared to the ministry of the local pastor with creeds and forms of worship to match, the evangelical faith relied for its authenticity on individuals' personal experiences and the encouragement supplied through the private gatherings of zealous believers. In nineteenth-century America this type of devotion became the most popular among Protestants. Unlike England, where the established church still controlled and regulated religious life, in the United States the separation of church and state was a boon for religion of the kind evangelicals promoted. Without the barriers of ecclesiastical establishment or state supervision, evangelicals were free to adapt their highly flexible faith to an endless variety of settings, both in order to gain new converts and to nurture the converted. One of the great ironies of American Christianity is that the victory of secular arguments for religious disestablishment ended up providing the conditions in which evangelicalism could thrive.

The Roman Catholic response to modernity was very different than the evangelical Protestant one. Rather than turning inward, the Vatican defiantly reasserted its historic claims to primacy among the several powers of church and state. Rome's conservatism was catalyzed in large part by its experience during the French Revolution. The Civil Constitution of the First French Republic, which required an oath of loyalty from church officers, was devastating to Catholicism in France, leading to the execution or exile of thousands of priests. The anticlericalism of the French Revolution, combined with the democratic revolutions in nineteenth-century Europe, prompted the papacy to oppose modernity's innovations, from the rationalism of Enlightenment philosophers to the newly articulated principles of economic and political liberty. Arguably the greatest expression of the papacy's conservatism during the nineteenth century was the First Vatican Council, which met from 1869 to 1870. Among other things, this gathering of bishops defined the doctrine of papal infallibility, which holds that when the pope speaks or teaches in his official capacity on moral or doctrinal matters, he is protected by the Holy Spirit from doing so in error.

As reactionary as Roman Catholicism appeared to Protestants and the West's champions of liberal democracy, the papacy's opposition to modernity was usually thoughtful. The careful reflections of several popes can be found in a string of encyclicals on such diverse topics as the plight of industrial laborers and biblical interpretation. In addition, a number of Roman Catholic intellectuals offered important critiques of modernity while also contending that, if premised upon Catholic teaching, the better aspects of modern thought concerning freedom and society could be salvaged and used for humane ends. For instance, England's Cardinal John Henry Newman (1801–90) argued in *The Idea of a University* (1854) for the centrality of theology in human knowing rightly understood. In a similar fashion, the American Orestes Brownson (1803–76) attempted to show in *The American Republic* (1865) that democracy would flourish only when embedded in the context of Roman Catholic notions of order and authority. More recently, neoscholastic philosophers such as Jacques Maritain (1882–1972) and Etienne Gilson (1884–1978) applied fruitfully the teachings of Aquinas to twentieth-century academic debates about the need for metaphysical considerations in scientific and historical investigation.

After World War II the stance of the papacy regarding modernity began to soften. This shift culminated in the Second Vatican Council, which met from 1962 to 1967 and sought to define how the church ought to engage modern culture. Its two most notable statements reflected a subtler, and certainly more hopeful, approach to the ideals of democracy and freedom: *Dignitatis Humanae,* for example, affirmed the principle of religious liberty for all peoples, while *Gaudium et Spes* redefined the role of the church's ministry in a world that had been thoroughly secularized. The cumulative effect of the Second Vatican Council was to shift the papacy's stance from that of resistance to one of seeking both to identify and cultivate the best features of modern social arrangements and cultural expressions. The social and political unrest that bedeviled the 1960s—

including the Catholic Church—undermined some of the church's optimism about modernity, but the new attitude exhibited in the Second Vatican Council's documents, combined with John Paul II's papacy, invigorated Roman Catholicism and established the church as a source of wisdom on some of the modern West's most pressing political questions.

Ironically, though faithful to the work of the council and often themselves directly involved in it, prominent and insightful orthodox Catholic theologians—including Hans Urs von Balthasar (1905–88), Henri de Lubac (1896–1991), Karol Wojtyla (the future Pope John Paul II; 1920–2005), and Josef Ratzinger (now Pope Benedict XVI; 1927–   )—produced a body of work during the late twentieth century that served to deepen the church's critique of modernity while attempting to pave the way for an authentic *post*modernism in which the Gospel might again find a hearing. Ecclesiology, the relationship between nature and grace, and the human person became three of the favored loci of theological reflection. The *Ressourcement* movement, taking its name from the French word meaning "back to the sources," attempted to move beyond the limitations, rigid categories, and implicit modernism of neo-Thomism to recover the teachings of the early church fathers. Balthasar, an astonishingly prolific German-speaking Swiss theologian, exerted his greatest influence through his seven-volume *Glory of the Lord: A Theological Aesthetics* (1967–69), which made beauty the organizing principle for theological reflection. He was closely linked to de Lubac, a French theologian whose most important work, *The Mystery of the Supernatural* (London, 1967), argued for an understanding of natural law in which the revealed truths of nature were not conceived as extrinsic to divine revelation. John Paul II illustrated the subtlety and range of the thinking associated with the *Ressourcement* movement. His greatest intellectual contribution is arguably his theology of the body, explored in such books as *Love and Responsibility* (1993) and *The Theology of the Body According to John Paul II* (1997). In this teaching the pope creatively combined the church's historic teachings on sex, marriage, and the family with the philosophy of phenomenology to argue that Catholic convictions correspond to what it truly means to be human. More theologically (rather than philosophically) oriented than was John Paul II, Pope Benedict XVI is closely associated with the Communio school of theology, which is itself closely tied to the *Ressourcement* movement. Communio theologians have distinguished themselves in part by returning to patristic sources as a way of deemphasizing the strong emphasis on the independence of nature taught by some modern neo-Thomists. In the United States, their most important representative is David L. Schindler, whose *Heart of the World: Center of the Church: Communio Ecclesiology, Liberalism, and Liberation* (1996) is a detailed critique of liberalism and those Catholic thinkers who have proposed that it is fundamentally compatible with Catholic social and moral teaching.

The most prominent of those thinkers in America since Vatican II is John Courtney Murray (1904–67), who taught at the Jesuit school in Woodstock, Maryland, from which post he exerted a large influence on the church's understanding of church-state relations. In *We Hold These Truths: Catholic Reflections on the American Proposition* (London, 1960), Murray unfolded a way of regarding the American polity that aimed to harmonize modern political theories with Roman Catholic teaching. Though his views also elicited opposition initially from Rome, Murray's ideas were a significant influence on the Second Vatican Council's declarations. Murray's arguments on the compatibility between Roman Catholicism and liberal democracy have been kept alive with some vigor in the writings and activities of Richard John Neuhaus (1936–), for over a decade the director of the Institute on Religion and Public Life and editor in chief of the institute's journal, *First Things.* While still a Lutheran pastor, Neuhaus wrote *The Naked Public Square* (1984), a book widely acclaimed for its critique of liberal democracy uprooted from its religious soil. With *The Catholic Moment* (1990), an indication of his eventual conversion to Catholicism, Neuhaus argued that the best hope for evangelization and cultural transformation in the United States was the Roman Catholic Church.

Protestantism developed its own brand of conservatism, which in the nineteenth century developed not primarily in opposition to modernity but through the new circumstances afforded by it. Confessional Protestantism emerged primarily among American Lutherans, Reformed, and Presbyterians who, in opposition to the religious novelty of revivalism and through the autonomy afforded by religious disestablishment, sought to recover the original convictions and practices of their respective denominations. The word *confessional* narrowly signifies a return to the creeds and confessions of the Protestant churches (the Book of Concord for Lutherans, the Westminster Standards for

Presbyterians, and the Heidelberg Catechism for Reformed Protestants). But confessional Protestantism involved more than simply reasserting the truths taught in the various creeds and catechisms. It also included a recovery of the institutional church's importance. As such, confessional Protestants defended the prerogatives of the clergy, stressed the importance of the sacraments and liturgy, and opposed developments that had led their denominations to abandon the distinctive teachings of Luther and Calvin. The leading American voices of confessional Protestantism were John Williamson Nevin (1803–86), a professor of theology at Mercersburg Seminary of the German Reformed Church, Charles Hodge (1797–1878), professor of theology at Princeton Seminary of the Presbyterian Church in the U.S.A., and Charles Porterfield Krauth (1823–83), professor of theology at Lutheran Seminary of the Lutheran Synod of Pennsylvania. Confessional Protestantism was not merely an American product, though the pattern of state churches in Europe restricted the efforts of self-conscious Protestants in the Old World. Wilhelm Löhe (1808–72) led a related movement of confessional Lutherans in Bavaria. The mid-nineteenth-century Oxford Movement in England, though not as jealous of the creeds' teachings as were other confessional Protestants, reflected a similar impulse to re-cover the authority of the church and its ancient roots.

A different response to modernity came in the form of liberal Protestantism, the most influential position for the largest Protestant denominations throughout Europe and the United States. Here the strategy was not to resist the new challenges to religious authority in the way that con-fessional Protestantism and Roman Catholicism had, nor to locate faith's authenticity entirely in the believer's inte-rior life, as evangelicals had done. Instead, liberal Protes-tants accommodated the challenges posed by modernity by situating the ongoing revelation of divine will within the progressive unfolding of human history. The father of Protestant liberalism, Friedrich Schleiermacher (1768–1834), a German minister and theologian, recast Christian teach-ing in a way that resembled that of the evangelicals. Schleiermacher insisted that the essence of religion was not in external teaching but resided within man's inner con-sciousness or feeling. Although this view sounded evan-gelical, Schleiermacher's status as a university professor enabled him to set the trajectory for modern Protestant theology. No longer would the theological task involve correcting the errors and abuses of the church. Instead, theologians needed to address the alienation of the modern secular world from Christianity.

In the wake of Schleiermacher followed a group of Protestant thinkers, known as liberals, whose chief effort was to defend Christianity's plausibility to modern man. Put another way, the aim of Protestant liberalism was to adapt Christianity to the truths and temper of modern life in its political, economic, and especially intellectual aspects. One way to accomplish this was to appeal, like Schleiermacher (who was greatly aided by Immanuel Kant), to human consciousness. Protestants such as Frederick Denison Maurice (1805–72) in England and Horace Bushnell (1802–76) in America argued that all knowledge, especially religious knowledge, was subjective. They adopted this view in order to shelter faith from the fallout of the quest for scientific certitude. Another way to accommodate Christianity to modernity was to subject the Bible to critical investigation (especially what was known as the "higher criticism") in order to salvage its spiritual truths from its incredible narratives, a practice undertaken with great force by such German biblical critics as David Friedrich Strauss (1802–74) and Ferdinand Christian Baur (1792–1860).

A similar strategy for defending Christianity's plausibility came from historicism. This approach to history, noteworthy in the work of German church historian Adolf von Harnack (1851–1930), emphasized the cultural conditioning of religious truth and justified the ongoing effort to adapt church teaching to the circumstances of time and place, especially modern circumstances. Yet another significant effort to defend Christianity's plausibility came in the writings of the German theologian Ernst Troeltsch (1865–1923), who believed that Christianity's claim to absolute truth had to be revised in light of other world religions' claims. Troeltsch nevertheless tried to defend the importance of Christianity, both for its relevance to the West and for its attention to the personal character of human existence. For some, these liberal Protestant defenses of Christianity were but a waystation on the journey to unbelief. For others, they became the only plausible way of remaining a believer in the light of modern scientific, philosophical, and historical knowledge.

In the twentieth century a different response to modernity surfaced among Protestant theologians, a response characterized by a reassertion of Christian claims and a rejection of modern conceptions of knowledge as normative for faith. The word *orthodoxy* began to be used with greater frequency and urgency. This was particularly the case in Karl Barth's work (1886–1968). If Barth was not the greatest Protestant theologian of the twentieth century, he was certainly the most influential. A Swiss pastor turned university theologian who taught at a series of German and Swiss institutions, Barth's thought was forged in the crucible of German Protestantism, which had become a puppet of the state. Barth's criticism of this situation eventually led to his opposition to the Nazi government, a stance that cost him his academic appointment and was articulated in the Barmen Declaration (1934). Barth's oppositional stance also fueled his own theological development, which took shape in his *Church Dogmatics* (1936–69), a thirteen-volume effort remarkable not simply for its length but also for its recovery of a theological method honed before the rise of liberalism. Barth's recovery of an older theological style was not merely formal. He also set out to explore historic teachings on the Trinity and revelation and did so in ways that insisted upon the uniqueness of Christian teaching over against human reason, science, and the apparent progress of Western society. Barth's theology became known, appropriately, as Neo-Orthodoxy.

Among American Protestants, Reinhold Niebuhr (1892–1971) was the most important Neo-Orthodox theologian. Niebuhr came from a German-American background and was a pastor for thirteen years before becoming a prominent figure among mainline Protestants when he accepted an appointment to teach theological ethics at Yale Divinity School. Like Barth, Niebuhr made his mark by criticizing the Protestant mainstream churches' baptism of American culture. He too insisted that divine purposes transcended national interest, developing these ideas in such influential books as *Moral Man, Immoral Society* (1932) and *The Nature and Destiny of Man* (1939). Unlike Barth, however, Niebuhr was an ethicist, and his writings accordingly examined social and political life more than theology proper. In fact, Niebuhr's writings had great appeal even among secular intellectuals, sometimes known as "atheists for Niebuhr." This curiosity was in part a function of Niebuhr's political realism, which acknowledged both the limits of moral idealism and the need for political leaders to choose between greater and lesser evils. The result was an American expression of Neo-Orthodoxy more pragmatic and concerned with the active life than the European version, which had sparked a resurgence of interest in formal theology.

More recent, and often more radical, efforts to assert the antithesis between faith and modernity have been perpetuated by ethicists in the United States and theologians in Europe. In the former camp belongs Stanley Hauerwas (1940–   ), an ethicist at Duke University who has challenged doggedly the cozy relationship between American Protestantism and liberal democracy in the United States. A prolific and provocative writer, Hauerwas draws upon Anabaptist notions of opposition to the ecclesiastical establishment and the use of physical force, and on recent developments in the understanding of the church as a polity with practices unto itself, to insist that the life of faith must be lived in constant opposition to the liberal understandings of tolerance and individual freedom that characterize modern society. The titles of two of Hauerwas's most popular books suggest the character and flair of his arguments: *Resident Aliens: Life in the Christian Colony* (1989) and *After Christendom? How the Church Is to Behave if Freedom, Justice, and a Christian Nation Are Bad Ideas* (1991).

A far less accessible but equally profound critique of modernity on the basis of theological assertiveness comes from the school of thought known as Radical Orthodoxy. Here, various Anglican theologians at British universities have employed the devices of postmodern literary theory and cultural criticism in an effort to show the inevitable outcome of secularism and to offer Christian faith as a better account of human existence. The most important works in the Radical Orthodoxy project are John Milbank's *Theology and Social Theory: Beyond Secular Reason* (1993); Catherine Pickstock's *After Writing: On the Liturgical Consummation of Philosophy* (1997); and Graham Ward's *Barth, Derrida, and the Language of Theology* (1995). Although the result of Radical Orthodoxy for Christian theology is uncertain and much in dispute, its critique of postmodernism on theological and even liturgical grounds represents a further outworking of religious dissent, begun by Barth, against the faith's subjection to modernity's norms of reason and individualism.

Finally, less prominent but not less substantial than the responses of Protestant and Roman Catholic thinkers to the modern West have been the contributions of Eastern Orthodox theologians and various Jewish intellectuals, many of whom—thanks to the pluralism of the modern academy—have directly influenced their Protestant and Roman Catholic counterparts. Alexander Schmemann (1921–83), an émigré from Russia to the United States who spent most of his career teaching at St. Vladimir's Seminary in New York and wrote insightfully on liturgy and the sacraments in works such as *For the Life of the World* (1964), applied Eastern Orthodox teaching to the modern situation by insisting that the distinction between the secular and sacred was a misconception obscuring the divine presence in all of creation. David B. Hart, another Eastern Orthodox theologian, follows the lead of Schmemann in *The Beauty of the Infinite* (2004) by arguing against postmodernism to show that Christian theology offers the only plausible account of beauty.

Twentieth-century Jewish thinkers have also added important resources to theistic critiques of modernity. Martin Buber (1878–1965), a German-Jewish philosopher who eventually taught at Hebrew University, is best known for his book *I and Thou* (1923). Buber believed that biblical humanism would finally outlive the promise of science and progress through its appropriation at personal and communal levels. More recently, Jon D. Levenson (1949–), a professor of ancient Near Eastern civilization at Harvard and author of *Creation and the Persistence of Evil* (1994), and Leon Kass (1939–), a professor in the School of Social Thought at the University of Chicago and author of

The Beginning of Wisdom: Reading Genesis (2003), have simi-
larly appealed to a form of biblical humanism in an effort
to make plausible the claims of the Jewish scriptures and
to demonstrate the impoverishment of modern liberalism's
conception of man and society.

TAKE WHAT YOU CAN GET

The field of religious studies is an anomaly within American higher education. As we have seen, it has never fit well

---

The most likely place to find courses on Christianity in the modern
era is in religion departments, though in any number of offerings on
this period in history, literature, and political philosophy, students
should find the opportunity to study religion, at least as a subject for
research papers. Otherwise, the literature on the various themes
included under the heading of Christianity and modernity is vast. To
begin, some consideration of the eighteenth-century revolutions in
France and America and the different outcomes for Christianity in
these nations should provide a useful orientation to larger themes.
Books by J. McManners, *The French Revolution and the Church*
(London, 1960) and Nathan O. Hatch, *The Sacred Cause of Liberty:
Republican Thought and the Millennium in Revolutionary New England* (New Haven, 1977), offer helpful starting points.

The literature on evangelicalism and the subjective turn of Protestantism is large, but W. R. Ward, *The Protestant Evangelical Awakening* (Cambridge, 1992), and Nathan O. Hatch, *The Democratization
of American Christianity* (New Haven, CT, 1989) are texts that will
help the student begin to consider the affects of modernity on Protestant Christianity. Individual biographies of evangelical leaders are also
valuable, such as George M. Marsden's *Jonathan Edwards: A Life*

into any of the accepted divisions of study, not the natural sciences, nor the social sciences, nor the humanities. That is because it involves the study of the seminary and divinity school curriculum, even when it was supervised by a local minister. But in the university, divine things have no accepted place. The problem is not simply modern intellectuals' hostility to faith or theology. It is even greater than the oft-mentioned battle between theology and science, faith and reason. The problem extends to the very meth-

─────────────

(New Haven, CT, 2003) and Stephen Tomkins's *John Wesley: A Biography* (Grand Rapids, MI, 2003).

Different episodes in the history of Roman Catholicism offer perspectives on the larger topic of Rome's encounter with modernity. Austin Gough, *Paris and Rome: The Gallican Church and the Ultramontane Campaign, 1848–1853* (Oxford, 1986) and John T. McGreevy, *Catholicism and American Freedom* (New York, 2003) are worthwhile. At the same time, T. M. Schoof's *Survey of Catholic Theology, 1800–1970* (Boston, 1970) brings into focus the larger picture of Roman Catholic teaching. Two thoughtful books that explore tensions between Roman Catholicism and modernity are James Hitchcock's *Catholicism and Modernity: Confrontation or Capitulation* (New York, 1979) and *Catholicism Contending with Modernity: Roman Catholic Modernism and Anti-Modernism in Historical Context*, edited by Darrell Jodock (Cambridge, 2000).

Confessional Protestantism is a topic not well known, but its outlines can be gleaned from such anthologies as *Lutheran Confessional Theology in American, 1840–1880*, edited by Theodore Gerhardt Tappert (New York, 1972), and *Romanticism in American Theology, Nevin and Schaff at Mercersberg*, edited by James Hastings Nichols

ods of modern learning, techniques that have no capacity to evaluate the claims of divinity. Even if modern scientists wanted to evaluate the assertions of faith, they would not have any empirical criteria to render such an evaluation persuasive, let alone definitive. In effect, religion is a subject whose assertions and meanings are generally incomprehensible to the patterns of knowledge that prevail in colleges and universities.

For this reason, the field of religious studies inevitably

(Chicago, 1961). D. G. Hart's *The Lost Soul of American Protestantism* (Lanham, MD, 2002) presents confessional Protestantism as a type of Christianity that has been neglected to the detriment of Protestantism's health in the United States. The Oxford Movement in Anglicanism receives unconventional treatment in John Henry Newman's novel *Loss and Gain* (London, 1848). More recently it has been treated by the sociologist John Shelton Reed in *Glorious Battle: The Cultural Politics of Victorian Anglo-Catholicism* (Nashville, 2000).

For the European side of Protestant liberalism students should consult Owen Chadwick's *Secularization of the European Mind in the Nineteenth Century* (Cambridge, 1975) and Bernard M. G. Reardon's *Religious Thought in the Nineteenth Century* (Cambridge, 1966). The American expression of liberal Protestantism is a subject that William R. Hutchison carefully unravels in *The Modernist Impulse in American Protestantism* (Cambridge, MA, 1976).

The twentieth-century turn in Christian thought to an oppositional stance against modernity is accessible mainly through the authors themselves. But the writings of the Neo-Orthodox theologians are sufficiently part of the past to assess their legacy. One might begin studying Karl Barth with Geoffrey W. Bromiley's *Introduction to the*

raises questions about the secularization of American higher education. The dominance of scientific approaches to truth, whether conceived as narrowly empirical or broadly rational, appears to allow little room for religious perspectives on the topics and methods of modern learning. And because the modern academy boasts of its tolerance for all points of view and the free exchange of ideas, the exclusion of religious convictions and teachings, whether arising from hostility or methodological assumptions, appears to con-

---

Theology of Karl Barth (Edinburgh, 1991). A more complicated read (as the title suggests), but arguably the best interpretation of the Swiss theologian, is Bruce McCormack's *Karl Barth's Critically Realistic Dialectical Theology: Its Genesis and Development, 1909–1936* (New York, 1997). Valuable treatments of Reinhold Niebuhr are provided by Richard Wightman Fox, *Reinhold Niebuhr: A Biography* (New York, 1985), and Ronald H. Stone, *Professor Reinhold Niebuhr: A Mentor to the Twentieth Century* (Louisville, KY, 1992). The writings of Stanley Hauerwas and the theologians of the Radical Orthodoxy and Communio schools have begun recently to receive analysis. For the first fruits students should consult *The Cambridge Companion to Postmodern Theology*, edited by Kevin J. Vanhoozer (Cambridge, 2003), and Tracey Rowland's *Culture and Thomism: After Vatican II,* which discusses both Radical Orthodoxy and Communio theologians with special attention to their respective analyses of modern culture. Although not simply a critique of Hauerwas, Jeffrey Stout's defense of liberalism in *Democracy and Tradition* (Princeton, NJ, 2003) does engage the ethicist's arguments at points that are especially important for considering the place of faith in liberal democracy.

tradict the university's claims to diversity and openness. Even worse, to ignore religion is to ignore the most profound questions about human existence.

In sum, the study of religion reveals important weaknesses in modern higher education. But although particular religious traditions, especially Christianity and Judaism, may plausibly argue for the right to be included in an education having any real claim to quality, the religiously plural setting of the modern university makes such inclusion a riddle without an easy solution. The best justification for the study of religion, consequently, is one that rests not on the superiority of the claims of a particular religion, assertions that science has no means to adjudicate. Rather, the best rationale for the study of religion is historical and cultural: which faiths have been most influential on Western civilization and culture? This question makes the inclusion of the faiths stemming from the Hebrew and Christian scriptures the most obvious way for colleges and universities to attend, if only by a sidelong glance, to the claims of these faiths.

Despite the various difficulties involved in the academic study of religion, students should not despair. As long as they approach those religion courses which are offered both within and outside the parameters of religious studies departments with the understanding that they likely will have their faith challenged as much as they will receive edification, that they will probably hear as much about the problems introduced by religious controversy and belief as about the positive contributions of faith, they should benefit from such study. And it is especially important for students to remember that for purposes of devotion and edification other institutions exist, such as the home, church, synagogue, or religiously affiliated student center. When balanced by the spiritual sustenance received from parents, religious advisors, pastors, priests, and rabbis, students should benefit from their critical engagements with the field of religion in the classroom. It is even possible that those engagements, to amend Augustine's adage, will lead to the understanding that is a crucial component of mature faith.

NOTES

❧

1. The older literature on religion and American higher education stressed the discontinuity between the religious orientation of the nineteenth-century denominational colleges and the secular outlook of the research university. For some of the most pertinent titles, readers should consult Richard Hofstadter and Walter P. Metzger, *The Development of Academic Freedom in the United States* (New York, 1955), Laurence Veysey, *The Emergence of the American University* (Chicago, 1965), and Hugh Hawkins, *Pioneer: A History of the Johns Hopkins University, 1874-1889* (Baltimore, 1960). The recent studies of this topic nuance the implicit secularization model of the older histories by paying closer attention to the influence of Protestants with liberal religious convictions on the new universities. The best examples of this interpretive shift are George M. Marsden, *The Soul of the American University: From Protestant Establishment to Established Nonbelief* (New York, 1994), Julie A. Reuben, *The Making of the Modern University: Intellectual Transformation and the Marginalization of Morality* (Chicago, 1996), James Tunstead Burtchaell, *The Dying of the Light: The Disengagement of Colleges and Universities from their Christian Churches* (Grand Rapids, MI, 1998), and D. G. Hart, *The University Gets Religion: Religious Studies in American Higher Education* (Baltimore, 1999). Another important stream of literature is the one arguing for the legitimacy of faith and religious motivation in academic inquiry. Here the following are particularly valuable: Mark R. Schwenn, *Exiles from Eden: Religion and Academic Vocation in American* (New York, 1993), George M. Marsden, *The Outrageous Idea of Christian Scholarship* (New York, 1997), David W. Gill, ed., *Should God Get Tenure? Essays on Religion and American Higher Education* (Grand Rapids, MI, 1997), and Robert Benne, *Quality with Soul: How Six Premier Colleges and Universities Keep Faith with their Religious Traditions* (Grand Rapids, MI, 2001).

2. The intention here is not to deny the cultural significance of Eastern religions. In fact, the study of the history, culture, philosophy, politics, languages, and literature of Asia, India, and the Middle East regularly involves the study of non-Western religions. But because this series of student guides is predominantly concerned with those disciplines responsible for understanding the heritage of the West, what follows will likewise concentrate upon the place of religion in Western civilization.

EMBARKING ON A LIFELONG PURSUIT OF KNOWLEDGE?

Take Advantage of These Resources & Website

The ISI Guides to the Major Disciplines are part of the Intercollegiate Studies Institute's (ISI) Student Self-Reliance Project, an integrated, sequential program of educational supplements designed to guide students in making key decisions that will enable them to acquire an appreciation of the accomplishments of Western civilization.

Developed with fifteen months of detailed advice from college professors and students, these resources provide advice in course selection and guidance in actual coursework. The project elements can be used independently by students to navigate the existing university curriculum in a way that deepens their understanding of our Western intellectual heritage. As indicated below, the Project's integrated components will answer key questions at each stage of a student's education.

What are the strengths and weaknesses of the most selective schools?

Choosing the Right College directs prospective college students to the best and worst that top American colleges have to offer.

What is the essence of a liberal arts education?

A Student's Guide to Liberal Learning introduces students to the vital connection between liberal education and political liberty.

What core courses should every student take?

A Student's Guide to the Core Curriculum instructs students in building their own core curricula, utilizing electives available at virtually every university, and discusses how to identify and overcome contemporary political biases in those courses.

How can students learn from the best minds in their major fields of study?

Student Guides to the Major Disciplines introduce students to overlooked and misrepresented classics, facilitating work within their majors. Guides currently available assess the fields of philosophy, literature, general history, U.S. history, economics, political philosophy, psychology, classics, and American political thought.

Which great modern thinkers are neglected?

The Library of Modern Thinkers introduces students to great minds who have contributed to the literature of the West but are sometimes neglected or denigrated in today's classroom. Figures in this series thus far include Robert Nisbet, Eric Voegelin, Wilhelm Röpke, Ludwig von Mises, and Bertrand de Jouvenel, with many more to come.

Check out www.collegeguide.org for more information and to access unparalleled resources for making the most of your college experience.

ISI is a one-stop resource for serious students of all ages. Visit www.isi.org or call 1-800-526-7022 to add your name to the 50,000-plus ISI membership list of teachers, students, and professors.